"YOU WILL BE MY WITNESSES"

P9-CLD-619

Saints, Prophets, and Martyrs

JOHN DEAR

Icons by

WILLIAM HART McNICHOLS

ORBIS BOOKS

Maryknoll, New York 10545

Founded in 1970, Orbis Books endeavors to publish works that enlighten the mind, nourish the spirit, and challenge the conscience. The publishing arm of the Maryknoll Fathers and Brothers, Orbis seeks to explore the global dimensions of the Christian faith and mission, to invite dialogue with diverse cultures and religious traditions, and to serve the cause of reconciliation and peace. The books published reflect the views of their authors and do not represent the official position of the Maryknoll Society. To learn more about Maryknoll and Orbis Books, please visit our website at www.maryknoll.org.

Published by Orbis Books, Maryknoll, NY 10545-0308.

Information about icons by William Hart McNichols is available at:
http://www.puffin.creighton.edu/jesuit/andre/

Queries regarding rights and permissions should be addressed to: Orbis Books, P.O. Box 308, Maryknoll, NY 10545-0308.

Manufactured in Spain.

ILibrary of Congress Cataloging-in-Publication Data

Dear, John, 1959-
  "You will be my witnesses" : saints, prophets, and martyrs / John Dear ; icons by William Hart McNichols.
     p. cm.
  ISBN-13: 978-1-57075-641-2 (pbk.)
  1. Christian saints—Prayer-books and devotions—English. I. McNichols, William Hart. II. Title.
  BX2166.D43 2006
  270.092'2--dc22
                          2005025701

You will receive the power of the Holy Spirit which will come upon you, and then you will be my witnesses, not only in Jerusalem but throughout Judea and Samaria, and indeed to earth's remotest end.

—Jesus to the first disciples
(Acts of the Apostles 1:8)

There are no final proofs for the existence of God. There are only witnesses.

—Rabbi Abraham Heschel

Have mercy on these souls and on your witness as I come to you, the Great Witness to eternity.

—Al Hallaj (his last words)

You are my witnesses.

—Isaiah (43:10, 12; 44:8)

Contents

Contents

Introduction

When Jesus rose from the dead, his first words to his stunned disciples were "Peace be with you." He showed them his wounds and then repeated his greeting: "Peace be with you." Luke tells us that after explaining the scriptures and salvation history, Jesus said to his friends, "You will be my witnesses." With that, he ascended into heaven.

This little book offers icons and reflections, not about the Risen Jesus, but his witnesses. Witnesses are those who testify from personal experience about what they saw or heard. The Greek word for a witness also means a martyr.

Like a witness who takes the stand in court and pledges to speak the truth, these Christian witnesses take the stand in the court of life and speak the truth of God. They tell us that God is alive and at work, that Jesus is risen and calls us to his discipleship journey of compassionate love, and that God's reign of peace and nonviolence is at hand, right now, at this very moment. Their lives of Christian witness speak about the redemptive life of Jesus, God's reign of peace and justice, and the Gospel path of compassion and nonviolence. In a world of war, injustice, violence, and nuclear weapons, such testimony often results in martyrdom—as Martin Luther King, Jr., and Oscar Romero demonstrate.

The Apostles, martyrs, saints, and prophets represented in these pages witness to the presence of God at work in their lives and in the world, and they come to us once again in the ancient Christian art form of iconography to offer their testimony. The Letter to the Hebrews explains that we are surrounded at all times by "a cloud of witnesses." This collection shows the faces of some of these holy witnesses. They urge us to carry on their Gospel mission of love and peace so that we, too, might witness to the Risen Jesus.

Icons as Witnesses

Icons are an ancient Christian art form that gained prominence over the centuries among the orthodox churches of the East as "doorways to the sacred." The original Greek word means "to resemble." For Orthodox Christians, icons "unite the visible world with the invisible world," linking heaven and earth. As such, icons are not an art form, but a spiritual experience of the Holy.

When iconographers "write" their icons, they spend a great deal of time in prayer, study, and fasting, and then they paint the images of their witnesses in such a way that the icons come alive. The images become spiritual encounters with living witnesses who dwell in the new life of resurrection, but who witness to us here and now in our own time. In these encounters, we do not look at the icons: rather, the icons look at us. They witness what we do. They bear witness to the Risen Christ and the living God, and in the process, they disarm us and lead us into the presence of the God of peace.

An icon, Thomas Merton once wrote, is "a kind of sacramental medium for the illumination and awareness of the glory of

Christ within us. What one 'sees' in prayer before an icon is not an external representation of a historical person, but an interior presence in light, which is the glory of the transfigured Christ, the experience of which is transmitted in faith from generation to generation by those who have 'seen,' from the Apostles on down. So when I say that my Christ is the Christ of the icons, I mean that he is reached not through any scientific study but through direct faith and the mediation of the liturgy, art, worship, prayer, theology of light, that is all bound up with the Russian and Greek tradition."

Henri Nouwen wrote that "icons are created for the sole purpose of offering access, through the gate of the visible, to the mystery of the invisible. Icons are painted to lead us into the inner room of prayer and bring us close to the heart of God . . . It is only gradually, after a patient, prayerful presence, that they start speaking to us. As they speak, they speak more to our inner than to our outer senses. They speak to the heart that searches for God."

And Sr. Helen Weier writes, "The profound beauty of an icon is gentle. It does not force its way; it does not intrude. It asks for patience with the uneasiness of early acquaintance. It asks for time spent before it in the stillness of gazing. More important, it asks the one praying to allow himself to be gazed upon by it. One must yield space within yourself to the icon and its persistent beauty. An icon is prayer and contemplation transformed into art. When exquisite art combines with prayer to become a work of worship and wonder, the art becomes sacramental. It manifests to us the God who breaks through all signs and symbols with truth."

The Christian Vocation to Witness for Christ

Every Christian is called to be a witness for the Risen Christ. The saints and martyrs in these pages gave their lives as witnesses to Christ and his Gospel of peace, love, and nonviolence. They summon us to carry on the Gospel mission as Christ's witnesses, to stand with the saints and martyrs to welcome God's reign of peace and love, to denounce the injustices of war and poverty, and to work diligently for the abolition of war, hunger, the death penalty, abortion, poverty, and nuclear weapons. This Gospel work stands at the center of the spiritual life.

The Christians profiled in these pages demonstrate the Christian ideal. St. Maximilian was such a luminous witness, for example, that the testimony he gave before the Roman judge, stating his refusal to kill for the Roman army, was read at every early Christian Eucharist for centuries. Jean Donovan was assassinated in El Salvador in 1980 for standing with the poor and displaced victims of U.S. warfare, witnessing to the suffering and death of the Latin American poor. Philip Berrigan spent over 11 years of his life in prison for nonviolent civil disobedience against war and nuclear weapons. He is a witness to the nonviolence of Christ and the call to disarm and love our enemies. Each such witness shows a different angle on the face of Christ and the Gospel call to love one another, serve those in need, resist evil, and make peace.

Fr. William Hart McNichols, the Witness of an Iconographer

"It is the task of the iconographer," Thomas Merton wrote, "to open our eyes to the actual presence of God's reign in the world and to remind us that, though we see nothing of its splendid liturgy, we are, if we believe in Christ the Redeemer, in fact living and worshipping as 'fellow citizens of the angels and saints, built upon the chief cornerstone with Christ.'"

My friend Bill McNichols is one of the world's great iconographers. He began painting as a child, studied art at Boston University and the Pratt Institute, and continued to paint while serving as a hospital chaplain to people dying of AIDS in New York City, a priest in various parishes, and an advocate for gay and lesbian people. In the early 1990s, he moved to New Mexico to study with his teacher, Robert Lentz, another popular iconographer. Bill has "written" over 150 icons, featured in three books: *The Bride* (with Daniel Berrigan); and *Mary, Mother of All Nations;* and *Christ All Merciful* (both with Megan McKenna). He shows us the face of Jesus, Mary, the saints, and the martyrs, and through them, the face of God, looking at us and inviting us to the new life of love, compassion, and peace.

"When I work, I have to get completely immersed in the person's life," Bill once told an interviewer, "and then allow the particular essence or feeling of that icon to overwhelm me. I go to work as I go to pray—waiting for God to come. I don't go in knowing and I don't go in with presumptions. I go in waiting. I think part of my whole life has been an Advent. That has been my spiritual life."

"When you are with that particular person in the icon," Bill says, "it's like having someone in your house. I try to put their spirituality, their gift to the Church, in the icon, so that when you look at it, you get more than one dimension of who they are."

Bill goes on to explain that "icons change you from within because they are a prayer. They can create an atmosphere inside you to receive something new from God. They plough the field, and get the ground ready, so that you can receive what God is doing next.

"I've thought a great deal about this connection between our lives and the lives of the heavenly images icons place before us, and I think what you gaze at, you become, not only what you eat and listen to, but what you see. St. Ignatius was brilliant in this way. We always say, 'You are what you eat.' But you are what you see, too, what you gaze at. North Americans spend hours in front of the television, like a new icon that we gaze at, and it glares back at us. Yet we do not make any connection with what it would be like to gaze at something that truly loves us and wants to bring us closer to God. We need to gaze at loving images, holy images that will return our love."

This book offers 32 icons by Bill McNichols, followed by my brief reflections about the saint and what we might learn from his or her witness to Christ and the Gospel. The saints are positioned in chronological order, so the book could be read straight through, or opened up at random to any particular saint. My reflections are only starting points. I urge you to look long and lovingly at the icons, to let them look back at you, and to use these icons as starting points for your prayer. The letters in the icons, following the long history of iconography, are in Greek, and usually announce the name of the icon, such as "Holy Maximilian" or "Holy Philip."

May these holy witnesses to the peacemaking Christ help you on your journey of peace so that you, too, may be one of his witnesses.

John Dear
Madrid, New Mexico

1 | Mary
(First Century, C.E.)

The first witness to Christ is his mother, Mary. She is a young girl living in a small desert town on the outskirts of a brutal empire when an angel appears announcing that she will become the mother of the Messiah, and that her child's reign will never end. She is told that the Holy Spirit will come upon her so that her child will be called "Son of the Most High." She believes and accepts her mission with an astonishing declaration: "Let it be done to me according to your word." With that, she gives her life to Christ. She becomes the first and greatest witness of all.

In Luke's dramatic account, Mary is portrayed as the model witness. In the Annunciation, we see her as a witness of contemplative nonviolence, sitting in prayer, dwelling in the peace of solitude, attuned, listening to the voice of God. Her encounter with the angel pushes her into the world. She moves into active nonviolence and sets out immediately to serve her pregnant cousin, Elizabeth. By reaching out to someone in need, by putting love into action, she offers a witness to the good news of Jesus' coming. That experience of active nonviolence leads her to proclaim the Magnificat, a manifesto of prophetic nonviolence. "My soul proclaims the greatness of God," she declares. "My spirit rejoices in God, my savior."

1

In this prophetic announcement, Mary witnesses not only to the action of God in her life, but to God's disarmament and active transformation of the world. "God's mercy is from age to age. God has dispersed the arrogant of mind and heart. God has thrown down the rulers from their thrones but lifted up the lowly. God has filled the hungry with good things and sent the rich away empty" (Luke 1:46-56). Mary announces God's revolution of nonviolence. That is why she is the first witness.

Mary has become a legend; her story, her very name, a living icon. But the four Gospels report little about her life. She gives birth to Jesus, witnesses his childhood and youth, hears his first sermon in the Nazareth synagogue, and arranges his first miracle. At the wedding feast in Cana, after the wine runs out, she instructs the waiters, "Do whatever he tells you." That one line sums up her life message. Later, she stands at the foot of the cross and witnesses her son's forgiving love, perfect nonviolence, steadfast fidelity, and painful death. She is there in the days of his Resurrection, and prays with the disciples in the upper room at Pentecost when his Holy Spirit comes upon them like fire.

Today, Mary remains the great witness who points us to Christ. Her image has been painted by countless artists and iconographers, under hundreds of titles. This beautiful icon bears the official name of the original thirteenth-century icon: "Andronicus Icon of the Mother of God, Consoler of Mothers." Like the original, Bill McNichols' icon has a story.

When word came that our friend, the great peacemaker Philip Berrigan was diagnosed with cancer and had only a few weeks to live, Bill stopped what he was doing, spent a few days in prayerful reflection, and painted this icon of the "Consoler of

Mothers" for Phil's wife, Elizabeth McAlister, and their children, Frida, Jerry, and Kate. During Phil's last weeks, the family hung the icon by his bed where he lay dying in their community, Jonah House, in Baltimore, Maryland. Mary kept watch over Phil, his family, and the many friends who sat with him. In those days, Mary became a witness again, calling us to take heart and stay focused on the Resurrection of her son. The original icon witnessed Phil's beautiful spirit and death, and the loving community of family and friends that formed around his bed during his last week, a twenty-four-hour circle of prayer, silence, and love. Mary was our mother, our consolation. She helped us to trust once again in her son, our brother Jesus, and to center our hearts in the new life of resurrection. In that faith and hope, we knew that we would see Philip again.

As we let Mary look into our eyes, and we look into her eyes, we find new strength to follow Jesus, to become, like her, public witnesses for love and peace. With Mary, we can pray the prayer of Pope John Paul II:

> *Great and Merciful God, Lord of peace and life,*
> *You have plans for peace, and not affliction.*
> *You condemn wars and defeat the pride of the violent.*
> *You sent your son Jesus to preach to those near and far,*
> *To gather people of every race and nation into a single family.*
> *Hear the single-hearted cry of all humanity:*
> *No more war, no more spirals of death and violence,*
> *No more threats against your creatures in heaven, on earth*
>   *and in the sea.*
> *In communion with Mary, the mother of Jesus,*

Once again we implore you:
Speak to the hearts of those responsible for the fate of peoples.
Stop the "logic" of revenge and retaliation.
With your Spirit suggest new solutions,
generous and honorable gestures, room for dialogue and
            patient waiting
Which are more fruitful than the hurried deadlines of war.

                                        Amen.

2 | John the Baptist

(First Century, C.E.)

Iconographer Robert Lentz called Bill McNichols' icon of John the Baptist one of the greatest of all time. A copy of it hangs in my hermitage in the New Mexico desert, where it inspires my work to build a campaign to stop the production of nuclear weapons in nearby Los Alamos, the birthplace of the bomb.

Bill McNichols painted this icon as a companion to his icon of Our Lady of Medjagorje, he says, because Mary first appeared in Bosnia on June 24, 1981, the birthday of John the Baptist, signaling a new advent, calling us to repent of the sin of war and to prepare for the coming of the Prince of Peace and his gift of peace on earth. It is based on a Russian icon that does not include the Jordan River or a dove. In most ancient icons, John the Baptist holds his head on a plate, as a resurrected martyr.

Notice the robes, the rocks, the river, the staff, the cloud, and the dove that announces the Beloved of God. But do not miss the gentleness, the long suffering, the fidelity, the face of one who has waited for God, served God, loved God, and announced God's reign. Here is the face of the first public witness, the face of a Christian martyr, the face of nonviolent resistance to imperial injustice.

Even before he was born, John leapt in his mother's womb when the pregnant Mary approached at the Visitation. Legend holds that he was sent at an early age to a desert monastery where he prayed and studied the ancient scriptures. The Gospel of John states that John was "sent from God" "for testimony, to testify to the light."

Several aspects of John's witness urge me to be a witness for Christ. First, when he is asked who he is, he answers, "I am a messenger, a voice in the desert crying out, 'Prepare a way for the Lord!'" (Mark 1:1-8; John 1:1-9). John teaches me that I, too, have to become a voice crying out in the New Mexico desert, telling people to prepare a way for the Lord. John's witness encouraged me to move to the desert, like the early desert fathers and mothers, to cry out to the nation, "Prepare a new way for the coming of the God of peace. Dismantle your weapons, practice nonviolence, and live in peace." New Mexico is the poorest state in the nation; it is number one in military spending and number one in nuclear weapons. Because Los Alamos continues to build nuclear weapons and other weapons of mass destruction, the Church here must learn from John the Baptist to cry out against the culture of war and call people back to the God of peace.

Next, John calls us to repent. He proclaims "a baptism of repentance of the forgiveness of sins" (Luke 3:1-20; Mark 1:4). He wants us to repent personally, to repent communally as a Church, and to repent nationally as the people of the United States. This call to repentance demands conversion not only from personal sin but also social sin, the systemic sins of violence, greed, oppression, war, and nuclear weapons. Just as he challenges the Pharisees to show the fruits of their repentance,

John challenges us to "produce fruit in keeping with repentance." He does not want us to work for war, support war, pay for war, kill in war, build nuclear weapons, participate in corporate greed, destroy creation, or allow millions to starve. Rather, he calls us back to Christ's way of nonviolent love, justice, peace, and compassion.

John then announces that "the reign of God is at hand!" He denounces the sinful, worldly "anti-reign" of greed and war, and announces God's realm of peace and justice here in our midst. He calls us to let go of every trace of violence within our hearts and to reject our complicity with the culture of war and greed. Only then can we welcome God's reign—humbly, gratefully, and with open hearts—as a gift given to us undeservedly, without reservation. Welcoming God's reign means preparing for it and living now in God's presence. Gandhi once said that when everyone on earth is disarmed and practices nonviolence, then God will reign on earth exactly as God reigns in heaven. Gandhi taught, like John the Baptist, that living in the reign of God requires complete allegiance and steadfast devotion to God's reign, and not to any earthly nation. When we respond to John's announcement, we no longer place our trust in America or in any other nation. Instead, we live first and foremost as citizens of God's reign.

Next, we notice that John does not announce himself. He is not an egotist or a megalomaniac. He does not draw attention to himself. He does not point to the emperor, the empire, the president, or the government. Rather, his attention is entirely focused on Jesus. In John 1:19-34, we read that John tells his disciples, "Look, there is the Lamb of God who takes away the sin of the world. I have seen and testify that he is the Chosen One of God." John points to Jesus. His life is a burning witness to the coming of Christ. When he sees Christ, he tells everyone what he sees. And he wants us to do the same—to look for Jesus, to tell others to look for Jesus, to help others see Jesus in our midst, and to point out the presence of Jesus in our world among the poor, in our struggle for justice, and in every act of nonviolent and compassionate love.

Finally, John tells us that he listens to the voice of Jesus, and, in doing so, his joy is complete. Although we do not usually think of John as a joyful person, he calls himself the best man, the bridegroom's friend "who stands there and listens to him and is filled with joy at his voice. I feel joy and my joy is complete. He must grow greater and I must grow less" (John 3:22-30). Like John, we, too, need to listen to the voice of our friend Jesus. We need to stand next to him and rejoice when we hear his voice. In the end, as we side with Jesus, our joy will be complete because we are with Jesus our friend. Like John, we desire to spend eternity with Jesus in his reign. Until that new day, we help one another by pointing one another toward Jesus.

If we announce God's reign and point to Jesus as John did, we, too, will be consoled and will rejoice. John was eventually arrested and beheaded by the brutal tyrant King Herod. If, like Jesus, we dare spend our lives denouncing our government's injustice and announcing God's reign of justice and peace, we, too, may suffer persecution, arrest, even martyrdom. But also like John, our joy will be complete.

3 | Mary Magdalene

(First Century, C.E.)

Mary Magdalene is the first witness of the Resurrection. As the most prominent of the many women who follow Jesus, Mary of Magdalene is mentioned first in every listing of Jesus' female disciples (Mark 15:40-41, 47; 16:1; Matthew 27:55-56, 61; 28:1; Luke 8:2-3; 24:10). She has been portrayed down through the ages as a sinner and a prostitute, but the gospels never describe her that way. They say only that she is healed and that "seven demons had gone out" from her (Luke 8:2). Although she has been misrepresented by the Church, all four gospels emphatically assert that she witnesses the death of Jesus on the cross (Mark 15:40-41, 47; Matthew 27:55-56, 61; Luke 23:49, 55-56; John 19:25) and the empty tomb on the morning of the first day of the week (Mark 16:1-6; Matthew 28:1, 6; Luke 24:1-3, 10; John 20:1-2). She is the first to meet the Risen Jesus and is sent forth by him to tell the male disciples the good news of the Resurrection (Mark 16:6-7; Matthew 28:5-9; Luke 24:4-10).

Mary is so devoted to Jesus and overwhelmed by her grief that after his death, she goes back to his tomb early on the morning of the first day of the week to clean his dead body. There, standing outside the tomb, she meets the Risen Jesus, but she

10

does not recognize him. She thinks he is the gardener. "Woman, why are you weeping?" he asks. "Whom are you looking for?" When he calls her by name, she falls at his feet to embrace him. In this icon, we see the foot of Jesus and the shock on Mary's face as she recognizes his voice.

As she begins to worship her Lord, Jesus stops her and sends her on a new mission. "Stop holding on to me," he says, "for I have not yet ascended to the Father. But go to my brothers and tell them, 'I am going to my Father and your father, to my God and your God'" (John 20:11-18). John records that "Mary of Magdala went and announced to the disciples, 'I have seen the Lord,' and what he told her." Mary becomes the first witness of the Risen Jesus and fulfills her mission to proclaim his Resurrection to the disbelieving male disciples. She testifies to what she has seen, and, as the first witness of the Resurrection, her testimony is completely dismissed and rejected. She becomes the "apostle to the Apostles."

Mary of Magdala is the symbol of all holy women in the Church. Today, her story has been resurrected, and her feast is now honored by women around the world who continue her mission to announce the good news of Resurrection to their clerical, sexist, dominating, patriarchal brothers. "He is alive!" these Mary Magdalenes tell us. "Believe in the Risen One! Live in the new life of Resurrection! Stop supporting the forces of death that kill the world's poor: stop practicing sexism and domestic violence; stop crushing women; and welcome the Risen Christ's gift of peace, justice, and equality."

We churchmen too easily dismiss the message of these Mary Magdalenes. Nonetheless, like that first apostle, churchwomen today continue to announce the good news of Resurrection to churchmen everywhere, whether or not the message is accepted. Because they have seen the Risen Christ, they will not relent. I hope and pray that one day we men will hear this good news of Jesus' Resurrection and renounce our sexism and violence. On that day, we, too, will become witnesses of the Resurrection. We, too, will discover the great truth that death does not get the last word, that our survival is already guaranteed, that we need not seek power or domination, that we need not oppress women, that we no longer can support war or injustice, that a new day has dawned, and that we are all summoned into the new life of resurrection peace. As more and more churchmen accept the shocking message of Mary Magdalene all over again, the institutional Church will be healed, reconciled, and transformed. It will receive the Holy Spirit in a new Pentecost of peace and begin to witness more publicly to the truth of Gospel nonviolence. Women will be ordained. The poor will be served. Enemies will be loved. Weapons will be disarmed. Injustice will be resisted. And the peace of Christ will be preached near and far to all the nations. Mary Magdalene's mission will be fulfilled, and the Risen Christ will live in our hearts.

Thank you, Mary Magdalene, for going to the tomb, for fulfilling your mission, for announcing the good news of Resurrection to a people stuck in the culture of death. May we welcome your astonishing announcement all over again and witness to the Resurrection as you did first.

4 | Andrew

(First Century, C.E.)

The first person Jesus calls to be his disciple is a young fisherman named Andrew. John's Gospel says that Andrew is a disciple of John the Baptist, the one who announces, "Behold the Lamb of God." With that, Andrew leaves John to follow Jesus. After meeting Jesus, Andrew returns home to find his older brother, Simon Peter. "We have found the Messiah," he declares. He then takes his brother to meet Jesus. According to Matthew and Mark, Simon Peter and Andrew live with their family in Capernaum and are fishing when Jesus first calls them to discipleship. Tradition also records that Andrew preaches the Gospel and is eventually arrested and crucified in the ancient town of Achaia. Today, he is honored as the patron of Scotland.

The icon of Andrew, "The First Called," celebrates the call to discipleship. Here Andrew stands as a wise old Apostle being blessed by the Christ Child as the early icons portray him. He stands before us and asks us to reflect on the call to discipleship we heard. What does discipleship to Jesus mean for us? How do we continue to respond to the call to discipleship? How do we bring others to Jesus? What price are we willing to pay for our discipleship to Jesus?

"When Christ calls a person," Dietrich Bonhoeffer wrote in

his classic work, *The Cost of Discipleship,* "he bids us come and die . . . The call goes forth, and is at once followed by the response of obedience. The response of the disciples is an act of obedience, not a confession of faith in Jesus. According to our text, there is no road to faith or discipleship, no other road— only obedience to the call of Jesus. And what does the text inform us about the content of discipleship? 'Follow me, run along behind me!' That is all. To follow in his steps is something that is void of all content. It gives us no intelligible program, no goal or ideal to strive after. It is not a cause which human calculation might deem worthy of our devotion. It is nothing else than bondage to Jesus Christ alone, completely breaking through every program, every ideal, every set of laws. No other significance is possible, since Jesus is the only significance. Beside Jesus, nothing has any significance. He alone matters. When we are called to follow Christ, we are summoned to an exclusive attachment to his person. Discipleship means adherence to Christ."

St. Andrew reminds me of Archbishop Oscar Romero who was assassinated while presiding at Mass on March 24, 1980. Romero became a beacon of light, hope, and peace to the war-torn, impoverished peoples of Latin America. He spent three years as archbishop calling for an end to the war, the killings, the poverty, and the violence. His life was a living call to conversion and discipleship. "Be converted! Be reconciled! Love one another!" he said in his homily one week before he was killed. "Once we are converted, try to follow the Lord," he said on another occasion. "We don't follow him as yet with perfection, but the effort to follow him is what makes a true disciple."

"To each one of us," Romero declared, "Christ is saying, 'If you want your life and mission to be fruitful like mine, do as I do. Be converted into a seed that lets itself be buried. Let yourself be killed. Do not be afraid. Those who shun suffering will remain alone. No one is more alone than the selfish. But if you give your life out of love for others, as I give mine for all, you will reap a great harvest. You will have the deepest satisfaction.'"

As we look at Andrew, we see the millions of people down through the centuries who were called by Jesus. We also see ourselves, summoned to take up the cross and follow Jesus on the path of love, nonviolence, and compassion. We see ourselves challenged to resist evil, denounce injustice, do good, make peace, love our enemies, liberate the oppressed, announce God's reign of justice, forgive those who hurt us, bless those who persecute us, and give our lives in love for suffering humanity. Like Andrew, we are called to be faithful to the call of discipleship to Jesus, to live and die in the footsteps of the nonviolent Jesus.

As we ponder this icon, we ponder not only his courage to say yes to that first call, but our own courage in responding to Jesus. Andrew summons us to hear that call, to say yes to the life of radical Gospel discipleship, and to be faithful to the nonviolent Jesus for the rest of our lives.

5 | Origen
(185-254)

During his lifetime, Origen was considered the greatest interpreter of scripture and Christian doctrine. He spent over twenty years copying the scriptures and writing about them. He taught that God the Creator can be known only through the life and teachings of Jesus Christ, and that through a lifetime of contemplative prayer and scripture study, we can attain deep knowledge of God and the divine mysteries. But Origen was controversial, too, and eventually his life was forgotten. Theologians have only recently recognized the importance of his contributions. Many now regard Origen as the most influential teacher of Christian doctrine in history.

Origen was the oldest of seven children. He was born in Alexandria in the year 185. When he was seventeen years old, his beloved father, St. Leonides, was arrested, imprisoned, tortured and publicly beheaded. Origen was deeply affected by his father and his death. His father spent a great deal of time teaching Origen that the highest calling in life is to follow Jesus. For the rest of his life, Origen longed to become a martyr like his father.

Origen became a great teacher who defended and hid his persecuted Christian students. For a while, he even went underground. He practiced a strict discipline of prayer, fasting, sleep deprivation, celibacy, voluntary poverty, and nonstop theological writing. Scholars estimate he published hundreds of books about scripture, literary criticism, apologetics, dogma, practical works, prayer, homilies, and every theological issue imaginable. He traveled relentlessly across the Roman Empire, and spent the last twenty years of his life in Caesarea in Palestine. He lived to be seventy years old. Around the year 250, he was arrested, imprisoned, and tortured during the persecution of Christians under Emperor Decius. He was released, but died in the year 254 from his torture wounds.

In his famous book, *Exhortation to Martyrdom,* Origen writes at length about the spiritual benefits of martyrdom for discipleship to Jesus. "If we wish to save our souls so as to receive it back better than a soul," he writes, "let us lose it in martyrdom. If we lose our soul for Christ's sake, laying it before him in dying for him, we shall achieve true salvation."

Bill McNichols sets this icon of Origen in Egypt, with the palm trees and hot sun in the background, and the flame of the Holy Spirit on Origen's forehead. Based on the Fayum portraits of the Greek-Coptic Christians painted in Egyptian tombs, this icon shows Origen reverently holding a scripture scroll with his clothing in one hand, and the chalice of the blood of Christ, indicating the call to martyrdom, in the other hand.

"It is all but impossible to overestimate Origen and his importance for the history of Christian thought," Hans Urs von Balthasar wrote in 1938. "To rank him beside Augustine and Thomas simply accords him his rightful place in history. None of the great Fathers of the Church, from the Cappadocians to Augustine and on up to Dionysius, Maximos, Scotus Eriugena, and Eckhart, could escape an almost magical fascination of the 'man of steel,' as they called him. Some were completely swept away. Jerome, when commenting on Scripture, continues to copy straight from Origen's pages. Basil and Gregory of Nazianzen, in their enthusiastic admiration, make a collection of the most fascinating passages from his inexhaustible works. Gregory of Nyssa was even more thoroughly captivated. The Cappadocians transmit him practically intact to Ambrose, who also knew and copied him firsthand. In fact, many of the breviary readings of Ambrose as well as Jerome and Bede are practically copied word for word from Origen. There is no thinker in the Church who is so invisibly all-present as Origen."

"His sin was to speak first among mutes," Thomas Merton wrote in his poem "Origen." He was hated, Merton wrote, because he taught that in the end, everyone in hell would repent and be forgiven. "Frightful blasphemy!" Merton writes. "He said hell-fire would at last go out, and all the damned repent. To that same hell was Origen then sent by various pontiffs to try the truth of his own doctrine. Yet saints had visions of him. He 'erred out of love,'" Merton concludes. "He heard all beings from stars to stones, angels to elements, alive crying for the Redeemer."

We need to recapture Origen's zeal for scripture, truth, sanctity, love, martyrdom and God. As we ponder this beautiful icon, we realize that he not only witnesses to Christ but offers Christ to us in the Word and the sacrament, that we, too, might become living, shining witnesses to the truth of Jesus.

Ὁ ἅγ MAZIMILIÁN

ΙΣ ΧΣ

* I WILL NOT BE A SOLDIER OF THIS WORLD. I AM A SOLDIER OF CHRIST.

6 | Maximilian

(274-295)

In the year 295, the twenty-one-year-old son of a Roman veteran publicly refused to be drafted into the Roman army. As a result, the young man was arrested and brought to trial. His testimony was written down in a document called the *Passio* and later recited throughout the African Church as an example of true Christian discipleship. His life and death became one of the great witnesses in the early Church. He preceded saints like Sebastian and Martin of Tours and modern-day witnesses such as Ben Salmon and Franz Jagerstatter. From Maximilian to Franz Jagerstatter, these witnesses gave their lives to the truth that we are not allowed to kill, no matter how noble the cause, no matter how urgent the political crisis, no matter what the empire, the junta, or the government orders.

"I cannot serve," Maximilian told the Roman court in the town of Theveste, Numidia. "I cannot do evil. I will not be a soldier of this world. I am a soldier of Christ."

"What harm do soldiers do?" the proconsul asked.

"You know well enough!" Maximilian answered.

The proconsul then ordered Maximilian to wear the emperor's badge—a leaden seal that soldiers and citizens wore around their necks. Maximilian regarded the Roman seal as idolatrous, and so he refused. He said that because of his baptism, he wore the "seal" of Christ, and that the emperor's seal would deface his baptismal seal.

The proconsul then argued that other Christians had joined the Roman army, trying to use that fact to prove that Christians could follow Christ and fight for Caesar as well.

"That is their business," Maximilian replied nonjudgmentally.

"Maximilian has refused the military oath through impiety," the proconsul said as he sentenced Maximilian. "He is to be beheaded." Maximilian was immediately executed and his body was buried in Carthage in North Africa. The date was March 12, 295. Maximilian's refusal occurred on the eve of the Diocletian persecution at the beginning of the fourth century, when Christians were exiled, arrested, jailed, tortured, and executed.

Maximilian's holy resistance and martyrdom before the Roman proconsul offers several lessons for Christians living today in the American empire.

First, Maximilian exemplifies the absolute refusal to support war, regardless of the consequences to us. He pointed to the bottom line of the Gospel of Jesus: We are not allowed to kill. We cannot fight for any army. We have been disarmed and called to the life of nonviolence. Maximilian is the patron of conscientious objectors to war. Following his Gospel logic, every Christian must be a conscientious objector to war. No Christian should join the military. No Christian should work for the Pentagon, its weapons manufacturers, or its nuclear laboratories.

Second, Maximilian exemplifies absolute obedience to the nonviolent Jesus, even to the point of death. Maximilian reminds us that we place our allegiance in Christ, not in our government, its leaders, or its military forces. We do what Christ says, not what the draft board, the president, or the judge says. We do not allow imperial leaders to explain to us the Gospel, discipleship, or morality. Even if we are threatened with imprisonment, poverty, or ridicule, we refuse to fight. We are not soldiers of this world. We are nonviolent soldiers of the nonviolent Christ. Maximilian reminds us of the words of Jesus as he faced condemnation and execution before the Roman procurator, Pontius Pilate. "My kingdom does not belong to this world. If my kingdom did belong to this world," Jesus said, "my attendants would be fighting to keep me from being handed over to the Judeans. But as it is, my kingdom is not here" (John 18:36-37).

Maximilian prefigures the testimony of St. Thomas More before he was executed, when he told the judge, "As a Christian, I wish none harm. I think none harm. I say none harm. I do none harm."

Third, Maximilian's example summons us to reject idolatry as he did by refusing to wear the emperor's seal. He calls us to place our trust and security in the living God and to obey the teachings of Christ even if it costs us our lives. This means that we no longer pledge our allegiance to America or its idols, but to Jesus Christ our Lord and Savior. From now on, we, too, have been "sealed" at baptism with perpetual service to Jesus, and we will never break that seal. We do not worship false gods or trust in our weapons for security. Our lives are focused solely on the living God and the Holy Christ. We place our trust and allegiance in Christ. As Dorothy Day explained, once we render to God what truly belongs to God, we realize that there is nothing left for

Caesar, his idols, his generals, his judges, or his warmakers.

Fourth, Maximilian could have run away and saved himself, but instead, he stood up publicly and proclaimed his allegiance to Christ. He offers a bold public witness for the nonviolent Jesus. His example calls us to stand up publicly and to proclaim our allegiance to the nonviolent Christ, to become public witnesses of Gospel nonviolence. Today, many people talk about Jesus but ignore his strict nonviolence to the point that wars, bombing raids, and injustices are committed in his name. Bold public witnesses of Gospel nonviolence are needed now as in Maximilian's time. Like Maximilian, we, too, must not run away, be silent, or avoid controversy. We have to speak out politically, against imperial war making, resist the culture of violence, obey the nonviolence of Jesus, and let our lives be disrupted, even crushed.

"The fruits of this good work will be multiplied a hundredfold," Maximilian said as they dragged him away. "May I welcome you into heaven and glorify God with you!" In the end, Maximilian forgave the judge and his executioner. Today he challenges us to forgive those who hurt us, persecute us, or would kill us. He invites us to take heart in the knowledge that if we follow Jesus on the path of nonviolence all the way to the cross, we also will follow him into the new life of resurrection, where one day, we, too, will welcome others home.

If we refuse to be soldiers of this world, as Maximilian refused, our lives will bear the good fruit of peace. As a result of our public witness, one day war, poverty, injustice, and nuclear weapons will be abolished and all will dwell in God's reign of peace. Every Christian will understand the nonviolence of Jesus, just like young Maximilian.

7 | Dymphna
(620-640?)

In January 2002, the child abuse scandal broke in Boston. The Church around the country was shocked to discover that thousands of young people had been abused by hundreds of priests over the past four decades. As news of the scandal spread, millions grew outraged by the cover-up conducted by Church leaders, beginning with Boston's own Cardinal Law. Grassroots groups formed, demanding accountability, reparations to the victims, and new structures and procedures that include lay people in all decision-making processes. Eventually, Cardinal Law resigned, but as Church leaders clamp down, the struggle for structural change continues.

Like many, I was heartbroken by the pain and violence suffered by so many for so long from those who were supposed to offer healing and protection. I apologize to any and everyone who has ever been hurt by a priest or the institutional Church. I join the "voices of the faithful" who call for structural change in the institutional Church so that no one is ever hurt again; so that bishops and cardinals can never again cover up these crimes in order to protect their status or reputation; so that privilege, domination, and control are renounced; and so that a new Church of nonviolence, healing, service, inclusivity, and equality is born.

The Church scandal opened the door nationally to the dark secret and painful reality of child abuse across the United States. Although thousands have suffered and the North American Church is undergoing one of the worst crises in its history because of its failed leadership, the crisis has shed light on an ancient crime, and the need to defend children and victims of sexual abuse and violence. The scandal challenges us to work diligently for the end of child abuse, domestic violence, the abuse of power, and Church corruption of every kind. We are called to practice the nonviolence of Jesus who said, "Whoever receives one child like this in my name receives me, and whoever receives me, receives the one who sent me" (Luke 9:48; Matthew 18:5).

The Irish Church has long honored a child martyr who was a victim of abuse. It also honors the priest who was killed trying to protect her. Their story inspires us to defend children from those who would hurt them, to give our lives, like Jesus, as Good Shepherds, protecting the flock against all forms of exploitation, violence, and abuse.

St. Dymphna was born in the seventh century. Her father, Damon, was a pagan chieftain of wealth and power. Her mother was a devout Christian who was admired for her physical beauty. Dymphna was instructed in the Christian faith by her parish priest, Father Gerebran (who also was canonized).

Dymphna was fourteen years old when her mother died and her father descended into mental illness. Because Dymphna began, more and more, to resemble her beautiful mother, her father began to stalk her and threaten her with sexual abuse. In fear and terror, Dymphna went to see Father Gerebran. "You have to leave here immediately," he said, and offered to take her out of the country. Along with two other parishioners, they fled to Europe and landed near Antwerp, Belgium, where they settled in the village of Gheel. There, she began a life of prayer and service to the sick and poor.

Over time, Dymphna's father went insane and became obsessed with his daughter. He tracked her all the way to Belgium. Because Father Gerebran had used Irish coins on their journey, Damon simply followed the Irish money to find his runaway daughter and the priest responsible for her escape. When Father Gerebran tried to defend Dymphna, he was killed by Damon's men. Then, Damon ordered his daughter to return immediately with him to Ireland to live as his wife. When Dymphna refused, Damon drew his sword and killed her. She was fifteen years old.

Dymphna and Father Gerebran died sometime between 620 and 640. A few years later, local Christians built a shrine over their graves. The news of Dymphna's story spread, and pilgrims came to pray there for healing. Within a short while, miracles were attributed to the young saint. Today, she is regarded as the patron saint of the mentally ill and emotionally disturbed, and remains popular for her defense of victims of sexual abuse and domestic violence.

Through the example of Dymphna and Father Gerebran, we find new strength to stop sexual abuse, domestic violence, and the exploitation of children. As we meditate on her icon, a symbol of all children who have suffered violence from adults, we hear the call to renounce our violence, to practice Gospel nonviolence, and to end the Church's silent complicity in the crisis of sexual abuse.

From now on, we teach and practice nonviolent sexuality. We defend the rights, dignity, and innocence of children. We work for the reform of the Catholic Church so that crimes and corruption are no longer covered up, so that the perpetrators are no longer in positions of leadership, and so that the Church becomes the community of nonviolence and healing that Jesus desires. Like Jesus, we welcome all children in love and peace.

Hallāj al Asrār

8 | Mansur al-Hallaj
(858-922)

In 1999, Kathy Kelly and I brought two Nobel Peace Prize winners to Iraq, where we met government, United Nations, religious, and relief agency officials, as well as thousands of school children and dying patients in the run-down Baghdad schools and hospitals. On our first night, the leading humanitarians hosted a dinner for us in Baghdad. Margaret Hassan, the British-born director of CARE and the most influential advocate for humanitarian aid, told us how U.S. sanctions and bombing raids had destroyed Iraq's water purification systems, killing half a million children, as UNICEF and the World Health Organization verified.

Margaret Hassan, who had lived for thrity years in Iraq, witnessed firsthand the suffering and death of Iraqis from U.S. bombings and sanctions. In the months after the 2003 U.S. invasion, Iraq spiraled downward into violence. Westerners faced kidnapping and execution. Then, in October 2004, Margaret Hassan herself was kidnapped. A month later, after appearing on several videotapes, showing her crying and pleading for her life and for Britain to pull its troops out of Iraq, she was executed.

I consider Margaret Hassan one of Baghdad's many saints

and martyrs. She obeyed Jesus' commandment to love our enemies. She stood with the victims of the war on Iraq, especially the millions of suffering children. Because of her solidarity with Iraqi children, and her refusal to leave, she was brutally killed.

Margaret loved Iraq and its people. She became a Muslim, and modeled the best of Islamic service and compassion. She recognized Iraq as the birthplace of humanity, where writing was invented in the Sumer Valley, where the Garden of Eden was portrayed as the land between the Tigris and the Euphrates, where the prophets—from Abraham to Jonah—lived and died.

Islam in general and Iraq in particular share many saints, martyrs, heroes, and peacemakers. One of the most controversial Sufi saints in Islamic and Iraqi history was Mansur al-Hallaj. The French scholar and peacemaker Louis Massignon spent forty-five years studying the life of Hallaj. Massignon published a four-volume study, *The Passion of al-Hallaj.* He thought Hallaj represented not only the best of the Muslim world, but the best of humanity. He concluded that Hallaj was a great witness to love and peace. His groundbreaking research established Hallaj as the cornerstone of modern Islamic studies.

Hallaj was born in southern Persia in 858, and had memorized the Qu'ran by the time he was sixteen years old. At eighteen, he left home, traveled to Baghdad, studied with a Sufi master, and then embarked on a holy pilgrimage to Mecca. When he returned, he began to roam the streets of Baghdad, preaching to the crowds and calling them to an ecstatic love of God. He understood the problems of people so well that word spread that he could "read hearts" and point anyone back to God.

In time, Orthodox Muslim leaders grew angry at Hallaj and condemned him. In reply, Hallaj said that he wanted to burn as a flame of love to God. Later, when he undertook a second pilgrimage to Mecca, and was denounced as a heretic and a magician, he fled to India and then China, where he spoke to thousands of people about the love of God. Back in Baghdad, he was inundated with hundreds of letters from people all over the Far East. As a result, the government became suspicious of him, and decided that he was a threat to its power. Hallaj was eventually arrested, tortured, and hanged in Baghdad in 922. He forgave his murderers, praised God, and died serenely. His head was cut off and his body burned.

Over time, Hallaj has become a saintly hero of legendary proportions. He advocated justice for the poor, worked healing miracles, spoke wildly about God's love for humanity, and was regularly denounced as a heretic. He was a poet who became known as the ecstatic "mystic pillar" of Islam, "the martyr of mystical love." Hallaj announced that he wanted to give his life in divine love for humanity, to practice "a transfiguring compassion for the suffering of the world." He was persecuted precisely because of his mystical claims, such as his insistence that "with one saint, God purifies 70,000 people every minute." In his most infamous statement, he announced "I am the Truth." Today, scholars believe he was simply explaining his oneness with the Creator and creation, the deep truth that every human being is united with a loving God.

Sufism was new in Hallaj's lifetime, and orthodox religious leaders were intent on controlling it. They opposed Hallaj's teachings and resented his popularity. For centuries, scholars condemned Hallaj. Today, some even wonder if he existed; others argue that the vehement condemnations prove his existence. According to an ancient written account of his last night in prison, he spent hours repeating the words "illusion, illusion," over and over again. Later, he repeated the words, "truth, truth."

Shortly before he was killed, Hallaj offered a prayer from his death row cell: "We are here, we, your witnesses. We are seeking refuge in the splendor of your glory, in order that you show us finally what you wanted to fashion and achieve, you who are God in heaven and God on earth. You bestowed on this present witness your 'I.' You wish me to be seized, imprisoned, judged, executed, hung, my ashes to be thrown to the sand storms which will scatter them, to the waves which will play with them—if only because the smallest particle of my ashes, a grain of aloes burned for your glory, assures to the glorious body of my transfiguration a more imposing foundation than that of immovable mountains."

This icon portrays Hallaj in prison the night before his execution. He sits on a dungeon bench with the name of God, "Allah," blazing on his heart, as he looks up to the "Seven Stages to God." According to the text, he prayed: "I cry to you for the souls who witness where I now go, beyond the 'where' to meet the very Witness of Eternity. I cry to you for hearts so long refreshed by clouds of revelation filled up with seas of wisdom. I cry to you for the Word of God which, since it perished, has faded into nothing. I cry to you for the inspired discourse before which ceases all speech by the eloquent and the wise. I cry to you for signs that have been gathered up by the intellectuals—nothing remains of them except debris. I cry to you—I swear it by your love—for the self-control of those who mastered the discipline of silence. All have crossed the desert, leaving neither well nor trace behind. And after them the abandoned crowd is muddled on their trails, blinder than beasts."

The Muslim mystic Hallaj invites us into the heart of the Gospel, to love our enemies. But he also summons us to universal love, to lose ourselves in the ecstatic, mystical love of God, so that one day we, too, shall meet the great Witness to Eternity and be transfigured in unconditional nonviolent love. May we pursue that selfless love with the same disregard to consequences as Hallaj manifested.

9 | Francis of Assisi
(1182-1226)

Francis came alive to me in 1995 when I attended a week-long international conference of eight hundred Catholic peace activists in Assisi, Italy. The presentations were excellent, but I was so overwhelmed by the beauty and peace that radiated from Assisi, that I skipped the talks, wandered through the churches, strolled through the streets, and hiked the nearby fields and hills. I prayed at Francis' tomb, meditated in the little chapel of the Portiuncula, which he built by hand, and toured San Damiano. Two years later, after a second pilgrimage to Assisi, I took the long bus ride to La Verna, the mountaintop where he received the stigmata shortly before his death. During those holy days, I understood anew Francis' life of prayer, poverty, penance, preaching, and peace. His prayer became embedded in me: "Lord, make me an instrument of your peace."

Francis embodies the Gospel journey from violence to nonviolence, wealth to poverty, power to powerlessness, selfishness to selfless service, pride to humility, indifference to love, cruelty to compassion, vengeance to forgiveness, revenge to reconciliation, war to peace, killing enemies to loving enemies. More than any other Christian, he epitomizes discipleship to Jesus. His witness continues to shine throughout the world.

detail

Francis was born in 1182 and spent a wild youth running around Assisi in northern Italy, until he joined the Crusades, became a soldier, and went off to kill people in battle. But he ended up in prison for a year, became sick, and went home to recover. There he underwent a conversion, and decided to spend his life serving Jesus.

One day, while praying at the church of San Damiano, the crucifix spoke to him and said, "Go rebuild my church which is falling down." Francis thought God wanted him to physically rebuild the collapsing church building, so he started making repairs on the church and other church buildings. But over time, Francis realized God wanted him to rebuild the entire Church around the world, through prayer, poverty, and peace.

Francis began to preach through the narrow streets of Assisi, saying *"Pace e Bene!"* meaning, "Peace and goodness to you!" Today, we might dismiss his greeting as sweet and quaint, but back then, he was laughed at and dismissed as a crazy fool. In those days, everyone was violent. Francis preached nonviolence, and in response, people threw rocks at him. For the first five years, he was ridiculed by everyone. He, in turn, blessed them, loved them, prayed for them, and eventually reconciled them with one another.

One day Francis met a man with leprosy and was so appalled by the disease that he turned away. Then he realized that Christ is present in the poorest person, so he turned back to the man and served him, even kissed him. From then on, Francis gave his life to those who were poor and marginalized. In the process, he decided to become as poor as possible, to wed "Lady Poverty." He slept outdoors and in caves, served those who were hungry and sick, led prayer services, and fixed broken churches. Others soon joined him, and the order of "Friars Minor" eventually was formed.

When officials demanded a rule for his order, Francis opened his missal three times at random to the words: "If you will be perfect, go, sell what you have, and give to the poor." "Take nothing for your journey." "If anyone wishes to come after me, let them deny themselves, take up the cross and follow me." These Gospel verses became his rule.

Francis knew up close the sins, domination, and corruption of the Church, but he loved it. He thought the best way to change priests and bishops was to call them to God. Once he was urged to condemn a priest who was living with a woman and their children. When he went to the family's home and met the priest, he bent down and kissed the man's feet.

Francis did far more than love animals, preach to the birds, and build the first nativity crèche. He renounced violence and war, and announced that he and his followers would be people of nonviolence and peace. In his most dramatic episode, he joined the Crusades, not as a warrior but this time as a practitioner of Gospel nonviolence. In 1219, he began a year-long, unarmed walk right through a war zone from Italy to northern Africa, where he managed to meet the Sultan, Melek-el-Kamel, the leading Muslim of the time. Before the meeting, Francis begged the Christian warrior commander, Cardinal Pelagius, to stop the killings and the wars. The Sultan was so impressed by Francis' kindness and gentleness, that he announced, "If all Christians are like this, I would not hesitate to become one." He offered Francis gifts and a large sum of money, but Francis turned it all down.

Francis' journey through the war zone to meet the Muslim leader is the equivalent of traveling to Iraq today. Instead of killing the Sultan, he loved the Sultan and proved himself a true practitioner of Gospel nonviolence. Cardinal Pelagius, on the other hand, reflected the culture's ongoing justification of war and killing, even in the name of Jesus. He was no different than the priests, military chaplains, bishops, and cardinals today who support war, the bombing of Iraqis, and the maintenance of weapons of mass destruction. He refused to hear Francis' call to conversion and nonviolence, just as many church leaders today refuse to hear the call.

According to Franciscan Father Richard Rohr, scholars now state that Francis' real crisis began on his journey back home. First of all, the crusaders wanted to kill him as a heretic, so the Sultan's soldiers had to protect him from the other Catholic warriors. Then, when he arrived home, the friars began to grumble. They did not like his "politics," his outreach to the Muslim enemies. Eventually, they turned against him. To press the point, Francis added to his "later Rule" that all friars are to love their enemies "as the Lord commands" (Chapter X and Admonitions). "Francis took the message of Jesus absolutely seriously, as if it were personally directed toward him," Brazilian theologian Leonardo Boff (a former Franciscan) writes. "He accepted it totally." Today's "rule," however, is: Refuse to love your enemies. Refuse to meet with your enemies. And always, always, refuse to support those who do love your enemies.

At a large gathering of friars, according to legend, Francis insisted that they were not to own anything, and that they were to beg for their food, serve the poor, and preach the good news of peace, "sometimes using words." Tensions mounted. The friars wanted to build houses, so they rejected Francis and his orders. They did not support his nonviolence or his voluntary poverty.

Francis was so distraught that he eventually resigned the administration of the order. He fell into a severe depression and walked off to a hermitage on the mountain of La Verna, where he spent his last years in solitude, prayer, penance, sickness, hunger, and sorrow.

Yet it was there, in that spiritual darkness, that Francis plumbed the depths of contemplative nonviolence. "My Lord Jesus Christ," he prayed, "grant me two graces before I die. The first is that during my life I may feel in my body as much as possible the pain which you, dear Jesus, sustained in the hour of your most bitter passion. The second is that I may feel in my heart, as much as possible, the excessive love with which you, Son of God, were inflamed to willingly endure such suffering for us sinners." He spent long days on the mountaintop reflecting on the martyrdom of Jesus.

One morning in 1224, a seraph with six wings flew toward him. Up close, Francis realized it was a vision of the Crucified Christ. All of a sudden, Francis was filled with both intense pain and a universal, sacrificial, unconditional love for the whole human race. Rays of light shot out from Christ's wounds and, after the vision, Francis discovered the stigmata on his body. After months of suffering, he asked to be taken back to Assisi where he died outside the Portiuncula on October 3, 1226. Recent scientific studies of his bones concluded that Francis suffered from both leprosy and starvation.

Bill McNichols first visited Assisi and La Verna on a snowy winter day. He thought about Francis in poverty, walking in the snow, freezing yet praising God for the snow. In the first icon, "St. Francis, Wounded Winter Light," Francis points to God in the snow with a reverence for nature. He is a beggar, suffering from the cold, bearing the wounds, gesturing in prayer, beseeching God for the gift of peace. He is not powerful, proud, rich, or violent.

The second icon shows Francis receiving the stigmata from the crucified seraphic Christ. The mountains of Taos, New Mexico, stand in the distance. This icon was commissioned by the Church of St. Francis of Assisi in Ranchos de Taos, New Mexico, which Georgia O'Keefe made famous by her paintings. It now hangs over the back door of the church, so that parishioners in the beautiful, historic church head out into the world thinking about Francis and Jesus.

"We have only just begun to practice the Gospel," Francis told his followers as he died. Today we hear Francis tell us to embrace simplicity and poverty, serve those who are poor and needy, live in peace and nonviolence, love one another including our enemies, spend our days in contemplative prayer, and be devoted servants of Jesus and his Gospel. "While you are proclaiming peace with your lips," he wrote, "be careful to have it even more fully in your heart." He once explained, "If you own possessions, you need weapons to protect them and so we do not own anything and we are at peace with everyone."

Francis' logic points the way toward personal, social, and global justice and peace. If each one of us practiced Gospel simplicity, voluntary poverty, and downward mobility, like Francis, we would share the world's resources with one another, have nothing to fear from others, and live in peace with everyone. If the whole world, especially the first-world nations, practiced the Franciscan ethic of social justice and nonviolence, hunger and warfare would end. The United States comprises only 4 percent of the world's population, yet it controls over 60 percent of the world's natural resources. It maintains the world's largest arsenal of weapons, including 20,000 nuclear weapons. If we applied Francis' Gospel ethic toward ourselves, we would return the natural resources to the world's poor; relinquish the world's oil fields to their rightful owners, including Iraq; dismantle our nuclear weapons; and live in peace with everyone. In the process, we would learn, like Francis, to trust the God of peace.

Francis is not just for the birds. His life example and witness hold the key to the solution of the world's problems. He may be the greatest of Jesus' witnesses.

"I have done my part," Francis said to the friars around him as he died. "May Christ teach you to do yours." May we do our part, like Francis, and become instruments of Christ's peace.

10 | Clare
(1193-1253)

The little church of San Damiano in Assisi where Francis heard the crucifix speak eventually became a monastery for his most famous convert, Clare, and her new religious order of women, the "Poor Ladies," or "Poor Clares" as they became known. Clare would have been a good, moral person, but Francis introduced her to Jesus, and that led her on the path of discipleship to the cross, which she holds in this icon. "Christ is the way," she once wrote, "and Francis showed it to me."

Clare was born on July 16, 1193, to a wealthy family in Assisi. Her father, a count, died young. Because she was deeply moved by Francis as he preached through the streets of Assisi, she refused to cooperate when a marriage was arranged for her. Instead, she sought Francis' advice and they became friends. In the middle of the night on Palm Sunday 1212, Clare and her cousin fled to the little chapel of the Portiuncula, where Francis cut her hair off to mark her new life of prayer and devotion to Christ. He received her vows and promised to care for her and her sisters like his own friars.

After a brief stay with the Benedictines, Clare settled in San Damiano. There she lived a monastic life of prayer, penance, hospitality, compassion, community, and peace. Word of her

decision spread quickly, and other women joined her. The community of the "Poor Ladies" lived on alms together in complete harmony. Like Francis, they owned absolutely nothing so they could learn complete reliance and dependence on God. While the Franciscan men quickly modified Francis' strict rule of poverty, Clare maintained a strict voluntary poverty for herself and her sisters. She was probably anorexic from her early years, so she would not let her sisters fast in excess. She did not like giving orders, so community decisions were made not by hierarchical obedience but through consensus, an enormous historical breakthrough in the male-dominated Church. She also publicly insisted that women and men were equal, and so women need not rely on men to survive. Instead of punishing wayward sisters, she insisted on forgiveness, which became "the hallmark" of her community of mutual love.

Although Clare faced great opposition from male Church leaders, the community of poverty flourished, eventually numbering over 10,000 members throughout Italy during her own lifetime. Her sisters were sent throughout Europe to serve the poor and sick along with the Friars Minor. When a group of Friars Minor was martyred in Morocco in 1221, Clare tried to go there as well so she could be martyred, but the community would not let her. Shortly before he died, the sick, nearly blind, and stigmatized Francis visited Clare at San Damiano, where he composed his famous hymn, "The Canticle of the Creatures" to "Brother Sun and Sister Moon." Eventually, Clare's sisters, Agnes and Beatris, and her mother, Ortolana, joined the order.

In September 1240, during the Saracen invasion of Assisi,

some soldiers climbed the walls of the convent to attack the women. Clare immediately prayed before the Blessed Sacrament, told the sisters not to panic, brought the Sacrament to the entrance of the convent, and gathered the women to pray before it. The attackers had a change of heart and quickly left.

Clare was the first woman in Church history to have her own rule for religious life approved. Two days after this long-awaited papal document arrived, on August 11, 1253, she died at San Damiano. She was canonized two years later and is buried in Assisi. When sick people were brought to her, Clare would make the sign of the cross on their foreheads, and they would be healed. Clare herself was always sick, suffering the damp confines of San Damiano. Tradition holds that the Christ child appeared to her three times in order to comfort her, because she lived so harshly and spent so much time meditating on his sufferings. She spent time every day meditating on the crucifixion of Christ. In this beautiful icon, Clare holds a jeweled cross, indicating the wounds of Christ and her friend Francis.

"Behold Christ's poverty even as he was laid in the manger and wrapped in swaddling clothes," she wrote to Agnes of Prague. "What wondrous humility, what marvelous poverty! The King of angels, the Lord of heaven and earth resting in a manger! Look more deeply and meditate on his humility, on his poverty. Behold the many labors and sufferings he endured to redeem the human race. Ponder his unspeakable love which caused him to suffer on the wood of the cross and to endure the most shameful kind of death. From his position on the cross, he warned passers-by to weight carefully this act: 'All of you who pass by this way, behold and see if there is any sorrow like mine.'

Let us answer his cries and lamentations with one voice and one spirit: 'I will be mindful and remember.'"

Clare invites us through this icon to behold the poor Christ and his cross, and to take another step on our journey to Christ through contemplative prayer, community, compassion, forgiveness, equality, hospitality, and mutual love. May we pursue Christ with the same steadfast fidelity as Clare.

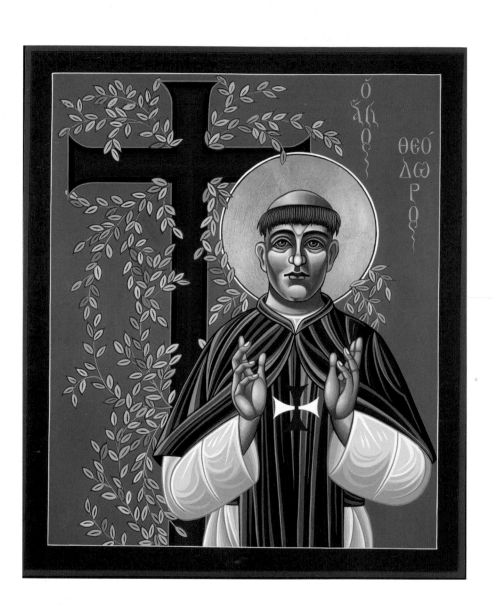

11 | Theodore of the Cross
(1166-1236)

Theodore of the Cross lived around the same time as Francis and Clare. He was probably born in 1166, but no one knows for sure. Like Francis and other Christians of the time, Theodore joined the Crusades and marched off to reclaim Jerusalem from "pagan armies." Over 100,000 men engaged in the crusades of 1187, but only 10,000 survived. Many died during battle or from starvation and disease. Theodore was appalled by the massacre of other human beings in the name of Jesus. Disillusioned by the Church's use of the cross as a symbol for genocide against Muslims, Jews, and others, he decided to dedicate his life to the formation of a new religious community centered around the cross as a symbol of love, service, and repentance.

In 1210, in the village of Huy in Belgium, Theodore founded the Crosiers, the "Canons Regular of the Order of the Holy Cross." His new religious order of priests and brothers lived in community, served the poor, prayed the Liturgy of the Hours, did penance on behalf of other clergy, and tried to honor the cross of Jesus. They wanted to practice the love, gentleness, and forgiveness of the Crucified Jesus. Not much else is known about Theodore, except that he died on August 18, 1236, and was later beatified.

Although they are not well known today, the Crosiers have over fifty communities around the world. On May 30, 1965, twenty-four members of the Crosier Order were brutally massacred in the village of Buta in the Congo. Rebels kidnapped them months earlier, bound them hand and foot, and eventually murdered them with lances and knives. "We are sad at the ignorance, ill will, and cruelty of the persecutors," the Order said in a statement at the time, "but we are grateful for the great charity, courage, and faith of these martyrs." Theodore would have been proud of his martyred brothers.

In this icon, Theodore invites us to take up the power and wisdom of the cross. He urges us to reject our modern-day crusades against Muslims, terrorists, and those who are different from us, and instead, to walk the way of the cross by practicing love, not hatred; mercy not revenge; compassion not condemnation; nonviolence not violence. He insists that the only way to reform the Church is through the cross. He calls us to undergo the cross, like his martyred brothers, not to put others on the cross; to be willing to be killed for the struggle for justice and peace, not to kill others; to sacrifice ourselves, not others, in pursuit of a more just and peaceful world.

The cross was a scandal in Jesus' time and in Theodore's time. It remains a scandal today. Instead of taking up the cross, we avoid the cross and put others on it. Instead of risking the powerlessness, pain, and failure of the cross, we seek power, glory, and success for ourselves and first world America. Instead of confronting injustice by nonviolent resistance, as Jesus did on the way of the cross, we support systemic injustice, and marginalize those who seek social change through active nonviolence.

In Jesus' day, the cross was a form of capital punishment used by the Roman Empire to execute revolutionaries and deter the population from resisting imperial injustice. When the early Christians used the cross as the symbol of their Way, they said, in effect, that they too were willing to be martyred. Theodore urges us to return to the cross of Jesus and give our lives as modern-day martyrs in pursuit of justice and peace for all people. He points us back toward the nonviolent, suffering love of the cross as the only way to social change and personal salvation.

When we give our lives for justice and peace in a spirit of nonviolence, forgiveness, and compassion, as Jesus demonstrated on the cross, our suffering love wears down our opponents, causes scales to fall from their eyes, opens up a greater recognition of our common humanity, and gives birth to social transformation, even the downfall of empires. Gandhi demonstrated the power of the cross when he used "nonviolent non-cooperation" and civil disobedience to force the British to leave India. Dorothy Day followed the way of the cross when she refused to take shelter during nuclear air raid "defense drills" in the late 1950s and suffered ridicule and imprisonment. Filipinos took up the cross when they took to the streets to protest the Marcos dictatorship and forced his flight to Hawaii, bringing about the birth of democracy.

Martin Luther King, Jr., was perhaps the greatest public proponent of the cross in recent decades. Throughout his countless speeches and sermons, he urged African-Americans to break the segregation laws, confront racism, demand justice, and risk imprisonment and even death for integration and equality. He knew that the suffering of an entire people would prick the conscience of white Americans. If nonviolence goes deep into the power of suffering love as Jesus demonstrated on the cross, King taught, it works. Justice and peace are the inevitable outcome.

"We will match your capacity to inflict suffering," Dr. King said, explaining the practice of the cross, "by our capacity to endure suffering. We will meet your physical force with soul force. Do to us what you will and we will still love you. We cannot in all good conscience obey your unjust laws and abide by the unjust system because no cooperation with evil is as much a moral obligation as is cooperation with good, and so throw us in jail and we will still love you. Leave us half-dead as you beat us, and we will still love you. We will wear you down by our capacity to suffer, and one day we will win our freedom. We will not only win freedom for ourselves, we will so appeal to your heart and conscience that we will win you in the process, and our victory will be a double victory." That is the logic of the cross, King explained. "Unearned suffering is redemptive."

"To be a Christian, one must take up the cross with all its difficulties and agonizing and tension-packed content," King taught, "and carry it until that very cross leaves its marks upon us and redeems us to that more excellent way which comes only through suffering."

If we pursue justice, truth, and peace, even to the point of suffering and dying in a spirit of nonviolent love, then we participate in the cross of Jesus and sow the seeds for a future of peace and justice. Theodore invites us to return to the wisdom of the cross, to take up the cross, and to carry the cross. He tells us not to be afraid of the cross or to reject the cross, but to embrace it as the way of God of social change. If we do, he insists, like Dr. King and Mahatma Gandhi, we will not only reform and transform the Church, but we will help abolish war and injustice. We will become faithful disciples of the Crucified Jesus.

12 | Ignatius Loyola
(1491-1556)

Ignatius looms large in the life of every Jesuit. For most of us, he is daunting, awesome, even a bit frightening. But I felt blessed to follow in Ignatius' footsteps in 1997 at the beginning of my Jesuit sabbatical year (known as "tertianship") in Northern Ireland, when I journeyed to the ancient Benedictine monastery of Montserrat, on a mountaintop near Barcelona. Ignatius went there immediately after his conversion, before his year-long retreat in a nearby cave and his journey to Rome, where he founded the Society of Jesus.

After a cable car ride to the mountaintop, tourists and pilgrims wait on a line to view the famous statue of the Black Madonna. Here, in 1521, Ignatius spent a night in prayer. Early the next morning, he took off his sword and laid it down in front of the Madonna and Child. He marked his conversion by literally disarming. From that moment on, he would be a nonviolent soldier of Christ. Then, as Ignatius left the shrine, he gave his expensive clothes to a beggar, put on the beggar's rags, and became a pilgrim for Jesus.

Ignatius was born in 1491 in the Basque country of Loyola, Spain, the youngest of thirteen children. He became a courtier, then a soldier for the Spanish king. During the battle of Pamplona on May 20, 1520, he was struck in the leg by a can-

nonball. Although he survived, he spent many months in painful recovery and walked with a limp for the rest of his life. During those months, he became bored and asked for something to read. The only books on hand were the lives of the saints and a life of Christ. He read them all and, in a matter of weeks, decided that he too should give his life to Christ and become a saint.

After his vigil at Montserrat, he spent a year in a cave near Manresa. As he prayed for hours each day, then reflected on his prayer, he noticed how he moved from desolation to consolation, from thoughts of suicide to feelings of ecstasy. With that awareness, he learned how to discern the presence of the Holy Spirit. As he meditated on the life of Jesus, he wrote down his meditations which, over time, became the basis for a groundbreaking retreat manual on spiritual growth and discernment known as the "Spiritual Exercises."

After a brief journey to the Holy Land in 1523, Ignatius went back to Spain to go to school. He formed a community, which eventually fell apart, and at one point, he was imprisoned as a heretic. During the next few years, he moved from Barcelona to Alcala to Salamanca and finally to Paris, where he completed graduate studies in philosophy and theology. There he met Francis Xavier, Peter Fabre, and other students who made the Exercises under his direction, decided to give their lives to Christ, professed vows with him in Montmartre in 1534, were ordained as priests, and journeyed with him to Rome, where he founded the Society of Jesus in 1540.

Just before he arrived in Rome to receive permission to found the Jesuit Order, Ignatius stopped by a small wayside chapel in the village of La Storta. There he had a mystical vision of God the

Father asking Jesus who was carrying the cross to "take this pilgrim with you." Over time, this seminal vision was meant to give all Jesuits the mission to accompany Jesus as he carries the cross for the disarmament and transformation of the world.

Ignatius became the first general of the new Order and spent the last fifteen years of his life composing the community's "Constitutions" and organizing the growing number of Jesuits. He spent his days writing letters to Jesuits and friends around the world. Some 6,000 letters survive. He also set up a variety of service programs around his headquarters, including a soup kitchen, a shelter for the homeless, and a house for prostitutes. At the time of his death, on July 31, 1556, over 1,000 men had joined the Order.

The Society of Jesus was revolutionary for its time because it was not a monastic community that required long hours of liturgical prayer. Rather, Jesuit priests and brothers were sent into the world to engage the culture, call people to conversion, and lead people deeper into the spiritual life. Jesuits were to spend only a short amount of time in prayer, attend daily Mass, and work hard for "the greater glory of God" by transforming people and cultures. Catholic missionaries usually traveled to other countries where they threatened people with violence if they did not convert. By contrast, Jesuit missionaries tried to inculturate themselves in foreign lands and point out how God is already at work in their culture, as with "the Reductions" in South America.

In the 1930s, Mahatma Gandhi dreamed of a "peace army" made up of thousands of trained, unarmed satyagrahis who could be sent on a moment's notice into the world's war zones to disarm and transform other cultures. Four centuries earlier, Ignatius tried to create just such an army of nonviolent warriors who would serve on the front lines of the struggle for justice and peace and help transform the world by welcoming the reign of God.

Ignatius wanted his men to undergo his "Spiritual Exercises," study philosophy and theology, be obedient to superiors, and pursue the "magis," the greatest good for the whole world. His Jesuit spirituality focused, first and foremost, on Jesus. Jesuits were to see life through his eyes, accompany him as he carried the cross in the struggle for justice, and become "companions of Jesus," "Friends in the Lord." Instead of turning away from the world, Jesuits were sent out to address and transform the world. Finally, Jesuits were to follow the lead of the Holy Spirit, notice the movement of Spirit in their lives, move from desolation to consolation, and help others "find God in all things." Ignatius broke new ground by inviting Jesuits and lay people to use their imagination to contemplate the life of Jesus and understand the nature of God. By calling us to imagine God as a God of love and peace, he helps us break free from our false gods to know and serve the living God.

This beautiful icon portrays St. Ignatius standing outside at night underneath the stars, which he loved to contemplate each evening. He lifts up his hands to open himself to God and surrender himself to God's will. The icon invites us to open ourselves to God that we, too, might give ourselves entirely to the God of love and peace.

With Ignatius, we can pray the concluding prayer of the "Spiritual Exercises:" "Take, Lord, receive all my liberty, my memory, my understanding, and my entire will, all that I have and call my own. You have given all to me. To you, Lord, I return it. Everything is yours. Do with it what you will. Give me only your love and your grace. That is enough for me."

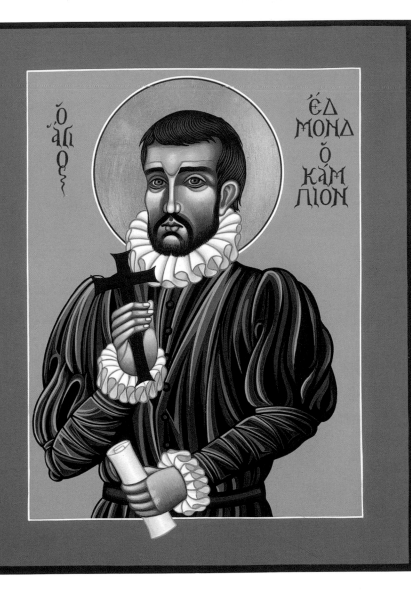

13 | Edmund Campion
(1540-1581)

The name "Campion" has become synonymous with the witness of martyrdom. Born in 1540, Edmund Campion studied at Oxford, where he professed the Oath of Supremacy, like everyone else, acknowledging the queen as the head of the Church of England. When Queen Elizabeth I visited Oxford, the university chose Campion, the brightest, most eloquent student, to offer the official welcome. In 1569, he moved to Dublin, and in 1571, he returned to England in disguise and converted to Catholicism. In 1573, he entered the Jesuit novitiate in Prague and was ordained in 1578. In 1580, he returned to England again and preached around London. He presided at illegal Masses for underground Catholics, and in 1581, he secretly published a statement in defense of Catholicism. When the statement was discovered by the authorities, Campion was hunted down, captured, and imprisoned. Apparently, he was offered his freedom if he renounced the Catholic Church and rejoined the Church of England. When he refused, he was charged with conspiracy and was tortured on the rack. Just before he was executed at Tyburn on December 1, 1581, he publicly thanked God for the gift of martyrdom.

We often look back on the Elizabethan world as a romantic

time of manners, castles, and privilege. In reality, it was an age of terrible violence and brutal inhumanity. Campion tried to lead Elizabethan England away from violence and oppression back to the values of the Gospel and the Church.

Campion's secret apologia, "A Challenge to the Privy Council," was disparagingly called "Campion's Brag." He offered to explain the Catholic faith before a wide variety of authorities, including the queen. The text remains one of the great documents of daring Christian witness. His mission, he wrote, was "to preach the Gospel, to minister the Sacraments, to instruct the simple, to reform sinners, to confute errors—in brief, to cry alarm against foul vice and proud ignorance, wherewith many of my dear countrymen are abused." He warned the rulers that Jesuits everywhere were determined to speak out, even to the point of martyrdom. "Be it known to you that we have made a league—all the Jesuits in the world, whose succession and multitude must overreach all the practice of England—cheerfully to carry the cross you shall lay upon us, and never to despair your recovery, while we have a man left to enjoy your Tyburn, or to be racked with your torments, or consumed with your prisons. The expense is reckoned, the enterprise is begun, it is of God, it cannot be withstood." His eloquent statement was widely distributed and threatened the authorities who feared it would inspire further resistance. All empires feel threatened in the face of such fearless courage, and they always respond in the only way they know how—with violence and execution—until the truth and suffering love bring them down.

Campion's witness challenges us in several ways. First, he is a bold truth-teller who accepts the personal consequences of his public truth-telling. In that sense, Campion is a prophet. He denounces imperial injustice and invites the government to convert to the wisdom of Christ. Such prophetic truth-telling is always politically costly. Yet in a "busy, watchful, and suspicious world," a world of lies, threats, and violence, the truth is needed most of all, along with fearless servants of the truth. We still need Christians who will give their lives in opposition to imperial might by announcing the truth.

Second, Campion practices what we now call nonviolent civil disobedience against imperial British rule. Just as Jesus turned over the tables in the Temple and questioned the ruling authorities of his day, so, too, Campion challenges the ruling authorities of his day, hides out from them, and publicly criticizes their injustice. Such illegal activity—the nonviolent civil disobedience on behalf of justice, truth, and peace—is a necessary requirement for Christians who seek to offer an authentic Gospel witness. From Jesus to Campion to Philip Berrigan, Christians practice nonviolent illegal confrontation with imperial authorities to proclaim God's rule over their false rule and to defend the poor from imperial oppression and the forces of death.

Finally, Campion models Gospel nonviolence by loving his enemies and even offering to meet with them. He proposes a serious dialogue and announces that he has already forgiven them for his inevitable execution. He even looks forward to spending eternity with them in peace. By reaching out to these imperial authorities, Campion offers a human alternative that could transform the culture of violence into a culture of equality, justice, and nonviolence. He demonstrates the Christian role in politics through the pursuit of dialogue and nonviolent alternatives on behalf of the common weal. Today, Christians need to put aside their violent fundamentalism and practice that same political, all-inclusive love by promoting dialogue and nonviolent alternatives for the transformation of our culture into a more just and peaceful society.

In this icon, Campion holds a scroll (his "brag") and offers us the cross. He looks at us solemnly, inviting us to take a similar stand today against the injustices of imperial government. He challenges us to confront the president, the Pentagon, and the ruling establishment, to brag about our allegiance to the nonviolent Christ, and to call for justice, disarmament, and peace.

We can carry on Campion's legacy by demanding an immediate end to torture and executions. We can denounce U.S. militarism, demand an end to war, and call for the protection of creation itself. We can point out our government's blasphemy against the Lordship of Christ, which is now worse than the horrors Campion faced in Elizabethan England, and requires the same steadfast resistance and willingness to give our lives.

If we challenge our government and practice the creative nonviolence that Campion demonstrated, we, too, may face harassment and imprisonment, but, like Campion, we will join the lineage of the saints and martyrs who witnessed to the trouble-making, truth-telling Christ, and be ready for "the day of payment" in heaven.

14 | Mary Dyer
(1611?-1660)

Mary Dyer was a devout Quaker who resisted the intolerance of fundamentalist Christians in the colonies of the New World until her execution in the Boston Commons on June 1, 1660. Her only crime was that she was a Quaker. She gave her life as a witness to Christ, calling us to show respect and tolerance toward one another, begging us to accept human difference and variety, and commanding us not to kill those who have a different understanding of truth. Her death challenges Christians everywhere not to kill other Christians. Her fearless faith summons us back to the nonviolence of Jesus.

Mary Dyer was born sometime around 1611. She and her husband William had six children. A Puritan, she became a follower of the well-known religious activist Anne Hutchinson who taught that God can speak directly to us, without the mediation of ordained ministers. The Puritans considered her views to be heretical. When Hutchinson was excommunicated by Boston's Puritans, Dyer stood by her side and publicly supported her. Subsequently, Mary Dyer and her husband were excommunicated and banished from the colony. They moved to Newport, Rhode Island, where tolerance toward other religions was practiced.

The Dyers traveled to England where they lived for several

years, and during that time, Mary Dyer became a follower of George Fox, the founder of the Society of Friends, known as Quakers. His teachings resembled the teachings of Anne Hutchinson. When she returned to Rhode Island, she decided she would visit Boston again to support her friends. This time, in 1657, she was arrested and imprisoned by the Puritan authority for being a Quaker. She was released when her husband promised that she would not speak to anyone until she had left the colony of Massachusetts. The following year, Boston officially banished all Quakers. It was illegal to be a Quaker in Boston. If any Quakers refused to leave, they would be arrested and hanged from the gallows in the Boston Commons.

In 1659, two of Mary's Boston Quaker friends were arrested and jailed. Mary felt she had to visit them, so she traveled to Boston where she was immediately arrested and imprisoned. That September, they were all released and banished, but told that if they returned, they would be executed.

Mary Dyer was determined to fight this injustice. A few weeks later, in the company of several friends, she returned to Boston to "look the bloody laws in the face." She was once again arrested and imprisoned. "Mary Dyer, you are to be taken to the place of execution and hanged until you are dead," the judge told her. "The will of the Lord be done," she replied. "Take her away," he said. "Yea, and joyfully I go," she answered.

She was taken to the gallows in the Boston Commons, where she watched her two Quaker friends as they were executed. Standing on the gallows with the rope around her neck, she received a last-minute reprieve. Against her wishes, she was brought back to Rhode Island. But she was determined to resist these vicious Christian fundamentalists, so she returned to Boston once last time, knowing she would be killed, in order to give her life for "the repeal of that wicked law."

She arrived in Boston on May 21, 1660, and was arrested. "I came in obedience to the will of God," she told the Puritan judge, "the last General Court, desiring you to repeal your unrighteous laws of banishment and death. That is my earnest request. If you refuse to repeal them, the Lord will send others of his servants to witness against these laws." "Away with her!" the judge shouted.

On June 1, 1660, she was led again to the scaffold on Boston Commons. She was offered one last chance to save her life, if she left and promised never to return to Massachusetts, but she refused. "Nay, I cannot," she told the crowd, "for in obedience to the will of the Lord, I came, and in His will, I abide, faithful to death." She forgave the executioners, explained that she was doing God's will, invited them to do the same, and spoke of the eternal happiness she was about to begin. With that, she was executed.

Mary Dyer hoped her death would lead to greater tolerance of all faiths. After the story spread of her resistance and execution, the King of England banned the execution of Quakers. A statue of her stands today in front of the Massachusetts State Capitol in Boston.

Mary Dyer's daring resistance and courageous fidelity even unto death challenges the growing fundamentalism and intolerance of our times and calls us to create a culture of tolerance, equality, and respect. She invites us to accept those who are different from us; to respect every human being; to treat every one civilly and nonviolently; to promote and defend civil and human rights; to resist unjust laws; to honor the traditions of other religions; and most of all, to follow Jesus by refusing to condemn or kill those who disagree with us and by inviting others to truth through compassionate love and the willingness to give our lives for one another.

Mary Dyer knew that Jesus associated with people who were ostracized and marginalized, that Jesus passionately wanted us to live in peace together with all people everywhere, no matter how different they are from us. May her witness touch us to overcome human difference and unite with everyone around us.

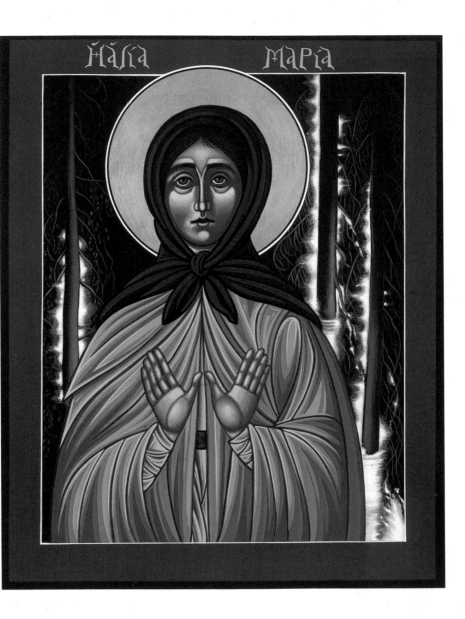

15 | Maria of Olonets
(1810?-1860)

Christianity has a long history of desert hermits, beginning with the desert fathers and mothers of the fourth and fifth century who retreated from society into the full-time life of prayer as the Church gave in more and more to the empire and its wars. In the 1960s, while writing prophetic essays against nuclear weapons, racism, and the Vietnam War, Trappist monk Thomas Merton moved into the nearby woods to live as a hermit, restoring a lost tradition to the Western Church. He withdrew from the culture of war in search of the God of peace as a service to the Church and humanity. His example helped lead me to my current life in a secluded hermitage in the New Mexico desert.

One of the most revered hermits of the Russian Orthodox Church is Maria of Olonets who was known for her disciplined life of prayer, penance, and solitude. As a teenager, she visited several monasteries and convents in search of her vocation, but always returned home disappointed, insisting that she could not join a monastery or a convent because they did not inspire holiness. In fact, she said they too often mirrored the world's problems. Instead of love, prayer, and peace, she found most religious men and women to be mean, jealous, petty, proud, and selfish. She did not see how their communal life served God's reign or led others into God's reign. She lamented that only a handful of people walked the long, hard road of prayer, penance, and peace to God and holiness.

Maria had heard about the Orthodox tradition of "desert dwellers" who lived alone in the cold, Russian woods as hermits, engaged in strict penance, poverty, and prayer. She decided to become a "desert dweller" in the northern forests of Russia, where she spent her life praying, doing penance, and weeping every day for the world's sins. Owning no possessions and suffering sickness and hunger, she spent entire days reciting the Jesus Prayer over and over again: "Lord Jesus Christ, son of the living God, have mercy on me, a sinner."

Maria modeled the life of prayer and solitude. But instead of finding support from nearby churches and monasteries, she was relentlessly persecuted. Her first two hermitages were burned to the ground by angry Christians, and the nearby male monks were jealous of her and harassed her. Who did she think she was, this single woman, living alone in the woods, spending her time in prayer to God on behalf of the world? Eventually, a niece and other young women moved close by, and she found some solace.

Toward the end of her life, Maria lived in a damp cave near Stavropol, where she endured the freezing cold of severe winter weather. She suffered a high fever, terrible pain, and ongoing exhaustion. After a long illness in the worst conditions, Maria died at noon on February 9, 1860. The nearby monks who waked and buried her later testified that her body radiated a glowing light. She became a symbol of prayer and sanctity for the Russian Orthodox Church.

In this icon, Maria prays alone in the woods with her hands

open to God. Notice that she stands slightly off center, just as she lived on the margins of the culture. We want to put her back into the center, but we cannot.

Maria of Olonets is a rare witness of contemplative prayer, penance, renunciation, and peace. She symbolizes every woman who dares to stand apart from the culture—and the cultural Church—in search of God. She enters into the woods looking for God, and discovers the hostility and violence of Christian men. People do not trust or support such serious devotion to God or the Gospel, then or now, but Maria remains determined to serve the world by standing apart from the world so she can focus completely on God and God's reign and repent of the world's sins. Her costly prayer is a great service.

Maria turns her back on money, possessions, prestige, family, career, power, and the world's illusions and wars, so that she can turn more freely toward the peace of holy solitude and plumb the depths of the spiritual life. Maria's witness reminds us that our lives belong to God, that each one of us should spend quality time in prayer with God, renounce our greed and violence, and seek God's reign of love and peace with all our hearts. May we pursue God with the same single-minded purity of Maria of Olonets.

16 | Bernadette of Lourdes
(1844-1879)

Like millions of other pilgrims, I made the long journey into the Pyrenees Mountains of southern France to the shrine of Lourdes. It was September 1997, and like other pilgrims, I waited on line to enter the healing baths beside the holy prayer grotto. When my turn came, several attendants led me into a tent with a stone bathtub filled with Lourdes spring water. After they prayed over me, they dunked me completely backwards into the water. I bolted straight up in total shock. The water was freezing cold! At that moment, I thought any illness could be scared away by ice water. Later, I presided at liturgy in the basilica, joined the candlelight evening procession, and climbed the mountain following the mammoth Stations of the Cross, all the way to the stunning Fifteenth Station—a large round boulder standing alone on the mountaintop, a vivid symbol of the empty tomb and the Resurrection.

I was not put off by Lourdes' famous tourist traps because I expected them. I was, however, unexpectedly inspired by the life of St. Bernadette. While standing in the tiny jail cell where she lived with her destitute family at the time of her visions, I recalled my own experience in jail for anti-nuclear demonstrations, and I suddenly gained a new understanding of this young woman. Such pain and poverty breeds utter dependence on God, and leads to a fearless witness of prayer, holiness, healing, and peace.

On February 11, 1858, fourteen-year-old Bernadette Soubirous and two other girls went to collect wood at a trash heap and pig sty near a stream and a cave. There in the grotto, she saw a beautiful, radiant young girl standing alone on a bramble bush praying the rosary. Bernadette prayed with her. Although her family and friends mocked her and forbade her to return, she went back ten more times to the grotto. During the third apparition, Mary said to Bernadette: "I do not promise you happiness in this life, but in the next."

Crowds followed Bernadette, skeptics criticized her, and her family was mortified. At one point, Bernadette was interrogated by the police, the court, and the bishop, but in each case, she held her ground. During one of the apparitions, Bernadette was told to drink from a "spring." When the crowd watched her drink a handful of mud, they realized she was totally insane. The next day, however, a spring of clear mountain water bubbled up into a pool in that exact location. The Lady asked for a chapel to be built on the spot and for prayer processions to be held there. It has since become the number-one Christian pilgrimage site in the world. Millions have prayed at the grotto, bathed in that spring water, and drunk from it. Hundreds have been miraculously healed there.

On March 25, 1858, the Feast of the Annunciation, 20,000 people watched Bernadette kneel in ecstasy before the grotto. When she asked the Lady her name, Mary held up her hands and said with humility, amazement, and even disbelief, "I am the

Immaculate Conception." Bernadette had no idea what that meant, so she repeated the strange phrase all the way home. When she told the priest, he knew then that the apparitions were authentic because no one in Lourdes, especially this illiterate little girl, had even heard of this obscure, new theological term. He himself had only recently heard it.

Throughout the apparitions and in the years that followed, Bernadette remained calm, faithful, peaceful, and centered. She retold her story hundreds of times. Although people were skeptical, annoyed, and jealous, her simplicity, innocence, and humility disarmed them all.

The last apparition occurred on July 16, 1858. Within a few years, Bernadette was brought to the novitiate of the Sisters of Nevers to live a secluded life as a nun in a large religious convent. The sisters, however, decided beforehand that they had to put this "celebrity" in her place. From day one, they put her down, were rude to her, and ignored her. They resented her lower class social status, illiteracy, and fame. Her superiors told her she was "good for nothing." Although sick most of the time, she served other sick sisters until her own illness forced her to stop. She suffered, among other things, a painful tumor on her knee. On April 16, 1879, after telling her story one last time, she died at the age of thirty-five.

From the day of her first testimony until the last day of her life, Bernadette endured the interrogations and hostility of relatives, friends, townspeople, police, priests, nuns, and bishops. Throughout it all, however, she remained steadfast and humble. Although her vocation was unusual, she fulfilled her role and became an instrument of healing, prayer, and peace. Bernadette is not flashy, despite her dramatic tale. Rather, her faithful witness summons us to simplicity, fidelity, prayer, poverty, humility, compassion, and holiness.

In this beautiful icon, eleven candles stand behind Bernadette, symbolizing the eleven apparitions she witnessed. Although she discovers the healing waters of Lourdes, she never uses them herself, even though she suffers constantly. She pours the healing water out because, as she said often, "It is not for me." Instead, she practices the kenosis of Jesus and empties herself so she can be filled with the Holy Spirit and serve only God.

Like Juan Diego who saw Our Lady of Guadalupe, Bernadette reveals how "God chooses the weak of this world to confound the wise." Her witness calls us beyond our own weakness, brokenness, and poverty to announce God's presence and action in the world. Like Bernadette, we, too, can announce the presence of God and call people anew to prayer, healing, and peace.

17 | Gerard Manley Hopkins
(1844-1889)

Gerard Manley Hopkins lived a quiet, hidden life as a Jesuit priest and high school teacher in England and Ireland until his death in 1889. Four decades later, his first collection of poetry was published, and by the centenary of his death, Hopkins was ranked as one of the greatest poets of the nineteenth century, maybe of all time. Like his contemporaries Emily Dickinson and Vincent Van Gogh, Hopkins became world famous only after his death. His witness to the presence of Christ in creation through his complex, fascinating poetry lives on and continues to inspire countless readers.

Hopkins was born on July 28, 1844, in Stratford, England. A sensitive, solitary young man with a curious intellect, he attended Oxford University, where he studied literature and dabbled in poetry. There he met the recent Catholic convert John Henry Newman. Under Newman's influence, Hopkins converted to Roman Catholicism, much to the chagrin of his family and friends. They were shocked even more when he entered the Jesuit novitiate and promptly renounced poetry forever so he could give his life entirely to God.

A few years later, on December 7, 1875, a passenger ship sank off the coast of England. Everyone drowned, including five

Franciscan nuns who were on their way to America. The local Jesuit superior said in passing that someone ought to write a poem about the tragedy. Hopkins took that comment as a sign from God to resume his poetry. "The Wreck of the Deutschland" is considered to be his masterpiece:

Thou mastering me
God! giver of breath and bread;
World's strand, sway of the sea;
Lord of living and dead;
Thou hast bound bones and veins in me, fastened me flesh,
And after it almost unmade, what with dread,
Thy doing: and dost thou touch me afresh?
Over again I feel thy finger and find thee.

With his famous conclusion, "Let him easter in us," Hopkins took up poetry again to point to Christ in the world. Although his poems were never published during his lifetime, they matured with themes of nature, weather, flowers, sky, earth, and the divine, to the point that some suggest he reinvented poetry and the English language. In the years that followed, as he worked in parishes and high schools from Liverpool to Dublin, Hopkins wrote of green landscapes and the spiritual landscape within, which he called "inscape." His poems celebrated earth and life, the natural and the spiritual world:

The world is charged with the grandeur of God.
. . . nature is never spent;
There lives the dearest freshness deep down things;

Ὅ ἅῃὁ

ΙΕ
ΡΑΡ
ΔΘ

And though the last lights off the black West went
Oh, morning, at the brown brink eastward, springs—
Because the Holy Ghost over the bent
World broods with warm breast and with ah! bright wings

In an autumn harvest, Hopkins saw the coming of Christ:

I walk, I lift up, I lift up heart, eyes,
Down all that glory in the heavens to glean our Savior;
And, eyes, heart, what looks, what lips yet gave you a
Rapturous love's greeting of realer, of rounder replies?
And the azurous hung hills are his world-wielding shoulder
Majestic—as a stallion stalwart, very-violet-sweet!—
These things, these things were here and but the beholder
Wanting; which two when they once meet,
The heart rears wings bold and bolder
And hurls for him, O half hurls earth for him off under his feet.

Pondering the Holy Spirit led him to write a hymn to peace:

When will you ever, Peace, wild wood dove, shy wings shut,
Your round me roaming end, and under be my boughs?
When, when, Peace, will you, Peace? . . .

While secretly writing poems, Hopkins carried on the drudgery of parish and school work. He was friendly, gentle, and perhaps a bit eccentric, but his classes and homilies were considered boring. He landed in Dublin, where he suffered countless hours correcting hundreds of high school papers and attendance sheets. He fell into depression, and the cold and damp air made him sick. "My go is gone," he wrote sadly. In a series of dark sonnets, he explained his despair, as on St. Patrick's Day 1885, when he wrote:

> *Thou art indeed just, Lord, if I contend*
> *With thee; but, sir, so what I plead is just.*
> *Why do sinners' ways prosper? and why must*
> *Disappointment all I endeavor end?*
> *Wert thou my enemy, O thou my friend,*
> *How wouldst thou worse, I wonder, than thou dost*
> *Defeat me? . . .*
> *Mine, O thou lord of life, send my roots rain.*

Even though Hopkins suspected his poems were good, he was resigned to failure. He sustained himself by pondering "the failure" of Christ, as he wrote in a letter: "Above all Christ our Lord: his career was cut short and whereas he would have wished to succeed by success, nevertheless he was doomed to succeed by failure. His plans were baffled, his hopes dashed, and his work was done by being broken off undone. However much he understood all this, he found it an intolerable grief to submit to it. He left the example: it is very strengthening, but except in that sense, it is not consoling."

In 1889, Gerard Manley Hopkins came down with typhoid. When the fever worsened, his parents were summoned. On Saturday, June 8, 1889, they prayed with him as he died quietly. His last words were his best: "I'm so happy, I'm so happy, I'm so happy." A day after his death, a relative walked by his bedroom and saw a Jesuit throwing hundreds of papers into a roaring fireplace. We will never know what great poems were lost in that flame.

There are many angles by which we can approach Hopkins and his poetic witness. He always seems fresh and original. Surely he was one of the first environmentalists. His Jesuit mission to "find God in all things" led him to embrace the "wild" world, a phrase that appears frequently his work. "What would the world be, once bereft of wet and of wildness?" he asks in "Inversnaid." "Let them be left, O let them be left, wildness and wet; Long live the weeds and the wilderness yet." He grieved the coming of the industrial age with its smokestacks and factories, because he knew it meant death for "the wild," and saw its deadly impact on his disenfranchised parishioners. He did not think factories meant the growth of "civilization," but the destruction of creation and our humanity.

In this icon, dedicated to Jesuit poet Daniel Berrigan, Hopkins turns his back on the industrial age and contemplates instead the kingfisher, the Holy Spirit coming upon him and creation. In doing so, he sees the presence of God, learns to recognize Christ in the face of others, and discovers his own true vocation—to be himself.

As we ponder the icon and the poem, we, too, discover Christ and our true selves:

> As kingfishers catch fire, dragonflies draw flame;
> As tumbled over rim in roundy wells
> Stones ring; like each tucked string tells, each hung bell's
> Bow swung finds tongue to fling out broad its name;
> Each mortal thing does one thing and the same:

Deals out that being indoors each one dwells;
Selves—goes itself; myself it speaks and spells,
Crying What I do is me: for that I came.
I say more: the just man justices;
Keeps grace: that keeps all his goings grace;
Acts in God's eye what in God's eye he is—
Christ. For Christ plays in ten thousand places,
Lovely in limbs, and lovely in eyes not his
To the Father through the features of men's faces.

18 | Thérèse of Lisieux
(1873-1897)

"When I sit in jail thinking of war and peace and the problem of human freedom," Dorothy Day once wrote, "of jails, drug addiction, prostitution and the apathy of great masses of people who believe that nothing can be done—when I thought of these things I was all the more confirmed in my faith in the little way of St. Thérèse. We do the things that come to hand, we pray our prayers and beg also for an increase of faith—and God will do the rest."

Dorothy Day, Thomas Merton, Edith Stein, Mother Teresa, and millions of others have pondered Thérèse's life and her ordinary witness of extraordinary love. Some dismiss her as a saccharine neurotic, but anyone who tries to practice her spirituality of sacrificial love quickly realizes how hard it is, how strong she was, and how transforming her personal nonviolence can be for all of us.

Thérèse Martin was born on January 2, 1873, to a middle-class family in Lisieux, Normandy, France. In 1889, at the age of fifteen, she entered the cloistered Carmelite convent, like her older sisters, and took the name "Thérèse of the Child Jesus and the Holy Face." She became the de facto mistress of novices, then contracted tuberculosis and died at age twenty-four, on

September 30, 1897, uttering the simple words, "My God, I love you."

Her death was unknown to the world except for the handful of nuns and relatives who knew her. She was considered a sweet, pious young nun. But when her autobiography, *Story of a Soul*, was published the following year, this young nun who never left the cloister exploded upon the Church. Within a few decades, she was canonized, celebrated as patron of France along with Joan of Arc, and eventually named a Doctor of the Church. A recent world tour of her relics drew crowds in the tens of thousands at nearly every stop. Today she is regarded as one of the most beloved saints of all time.

Thérèse appeared to live an ordinary life, but appearances can be deceptive. Life in a monastery is difficult. She dedicated herself to the daily practice of sacrificial love toward those around her, perfecting the art of responding to coldness, rudeness, gossip, and insults with active loving kindness and inner compassion. She aimed these small acts of unconditional love at Christ in the other person and for the redemption of the human race—a spirituality she called her "little way." She wanted to remain like a child, as Jesus instructed when he said that we must become like children if we want to enter the reign of God. She understood this spirituality not as childishness, but as a profound trust in God through confidence in God's love, not just despite our littleness, poverty, weakness, and brokenness, but precisely because of them.

Thérèse practiced a profound Carmelite spirituality of desert poverty and sacrifice, but her primary focus was love: sharing the unconditional, nonviolent love of Jesus himself. "Jesus, I ask

You for nothing but peace, and also love, infinite love without any limits other than Yourself, love which is no longer I but you," she prayed on the day of her profession of vows.

"My vocation is love!" she wrote toward the end of her life. While the Church around her was growing cold with power, rules, regulations, and indulgences, she was determined to be "love in the heart of the Church." Her mission was "to make Love loved," "to work for Your Love alone, with the one purpose of pleasing you, consoling Your Sacred Heart, and saving souls who will love You eternally."

Thérèse wanted to obey Jesus' commandment to love others as he loved, to love even one's enemies. In the Carmel, as she wrote, there are no enemies, but there are plenty of negative feelings toward others. There were many nuns whom she did not like, who offended her in small, petty ways, so she set about loving them as if it were a matter of life or death, no matter how small-minded, hostile, or cruel they could be. In June 1895, she formalized this commitment to active nonviolent love with a solemn prayer of oblation to God's merciful love. She would love everyone by allowing the love of Christ to consume her, share God's love with her sisters, and become a martyr of God's love. Many look upon such an oblation as typical nineteenth-century French piety, but I believe such steadfast love, united to Christ for the salvation of humanity, has the power to disarm the world.

Dorothy Day concluded her biography of Thérèse by comparing the power of Thérèse's Little Way with the atomic bomb. "Is the atom a small thing? And yet what havoc it has wrought. Is her 'Little Way' a small contribution to the life of the Spirit? It has all the power of the Spirit of Christianity behind it. It is an explosive force that can transform our lives and the life of the world, once put into effect." According to Thérèse of Lisieux and Dorothy Day of New York, the smallest act of willing love, united to the God of love, is more powerful than the atomic bomb itself, more explosive than a nuclear weapon. It is a spiritual explosion of love that disarms, heals, transforms, and reconciles.

Given our culture of violence and the world's wars, I prefer to translate Thérèse's spirituality as "the little way of nonviolence." Through these small acts of great love, we root out every trace of violence within us, allow God to disarm our hearts, and share in God's disarmament of the world. As more and more people practice this little way of nonviolence, love becomes contagious, wars end, and weapons are dismantled. As we organize our nonviolent love into direct public action, as Dorothy Day did, we can end nuclear air raid drills—and someday, nuclear weapons themselves.

This little way of nonviolence is revolutionary for it demands steadfast inner determination to confront the selfishness and violence within us, to open our hearts to be consumed by God's love, and to overwhelm those we do not like with good deeds, kindness, and loving service. Her example of taking the tough Sister St. Peter around in her wheelchair, preparing her food, and responding to her snappy remarks with a pleasant smile models interpersonal nonviolence for us.

Thérèse also exemplifies nonviolence toward ourselves. She refused to hate herself, put herself down, or fall into despair because of her own weaknesses and faults. Instead, she loved herself and practiced nonviolence toward herself. "If you are willing to bear serenely the trial of being displeasing to yourself," she wrote her sister, "then you will be for Jesus a pleasant place of shelter."

Thérèse wanted it all—to be a martyr, an apostle, a doctor, even a priest, but especially a saint. Confessing such desires was a radical act. "What pleases God is that God sees me loving my littleness and my poverty, the blind hope that I have in God's mercy," Thérèse wrote. "You can never have too much confidence in God, who is so powerful and so merciful. You receive from God as much as you hope for."

Thérèse's journey to holiness and active love inspires millions, but what is so intriguing about her life is that at the height of her devotion, Thérèse was plunged into a long night of disbelief. For the last eighteen months of her life, beginning on Easter Sunday itself, she lived through what she called "thick darkness," a "night of nothingness," where she was tempted over and over again to blaspheme God. As she suffered through the horrific physical pain of her final months, her heart widened to embrace all people everywhere, even unbelievers and atheists, with a profound compassion, though she herself had lost a sense of the presence of God.

"After my death I will let fall a shower of roses," she wrote. "I will spend my heaven doing good upon earth." In this icon, she clings to the image of the face of the nonviolent Suffering Servant, as the child Jesus clings to her. She showers us with roses, blessing us and interceding that God empower us to carry on her example of extraordinary love, her "Little Way of Nonviolence."

19 | Gemma Galgani
(1878-1903)

Gemma Galgani was born on March 12, 1878, at Camigliano in Tuscany, Italy. As a child, she suffered from tuberculosis of the spine. Her beloved mother taught her to pray constantly, and then died when Gemma was only seven years old. Although Gemma wanted to be a nun, she was not accepted into religious life because of her poor health. As a result, she spent her short life hidden away at home, suffering illnesses and poverty.

On June 8, 1899, like Francis of Assisi and Padre Pio, she received the stigmata and spent her last years bleeding and in pain. Mocked and humiliated, she remained focused on the passion of Jesus. She experienced mystical visions, revelations, and ecstasies; went to church every morning for two Masses; and attended vespers every evening. Throughout her sufferings, she maintained a spirit of peace and compassionate love toward everyone. She died on Holy Saturday 1903, at age twenty-five, and was canonized in 1940.

St. Gemma Galgani reminds us of the redemptive power of suffering love. "It is by suffering that one learns to love," she wrote. Her life challenges us to share the innocent, suffering love of Jesus, to accept suffering in the struggle for humanity instead of inflicting suffering on others, and to use nonviolent suffering love as a way to transform oneself and the world.

Gemma led a difficult, painful life. Death hovered around her at all times. But she turned this suffering around by plumbing the depths of contemplative prayer. Focusing her energy and strength on the Crucified Jesus, she became a witness of the suffering love of Christ. She teaches us that no matter what happens, no matter what sickness or disability or tragedy strikes us, we, too, can remain focused on Jesus through steadfast, contemplative prayer. We can find the blessing, the gift, the grace in any situation. Even in our brokenness, poverty, and powerlessness, we, too, like Gemma, can transform our lives and serve the suffering Christ with our love and peace.

In this icon, Gemma's heart radiates love. It is surrounded by a crown of thorns. She resembles the Sacred Heart of Christ who radiated perfect compassionate love as he suffered humiliation and death on the cross. With open arms, she invites us into the Sacred Heart of Jesus, to share his suffering love, to wear his crown of thorns, and to participate in his redemptive love for the salvation and transformation of the world. It is a difficult calling, but the goal of every Christian. We are summoned to accompany Jesus on the way of the cross into the depths of nonviolent love and the new life of resurrection.

"It is not enough to look at the cross, or to wear it," Gemma wrote. "We must carry it in the depth of our heart."

Gemma loved the cross of Jesus. "I do not refuse the cross," she wrote, "because if I refuse the cross, I refuse Jesus. I love the cross because I know the cross is on the shoulder of Jesus. It is on the cross, Jesus, that I have learned to love you."

In her faithful witness, Gemma calls us to stay with Jesus and to carry his cross with him. She wants us to love the cross of Jesus as well. "Together let us visit Jesus Crucified," she urges. "Let us not complain if we must stand at his feet. May it never be said that we could fail Jesus and leave him alone on the road to Calvary. Let us stay with him, even to the cross and death."

Love of Christ's cross is politically incorrect in our religiously charged times. But Gemma summons us to the heights of the Gospel, urging us to share her passion with the passion of Christ, to make the cross a reality in our lives by resisting injustice, confronting evil, and accepting the consequences. In the process, like Gemma, we too will experience of the depths of paschal love.

20 | Francisco Marto
(1908-1919)

The whole world knows the story of Fatima, how three young children had a vision of Mary, how the sun seemed to fall from the sky before tens of thousands of people, and how Mary urged people to pray the rosary.

But the story of the children themselves is not as well known. This icon portrays the boy Francisco, who, with his sister Jacinta and their cousin Lucia, beheld the vision. What touches me about this icon is Francisco Marto's radical insistence that we pray every day for an end to war.

Francisco Marto was born on June 11, 1908. According to the legend, Mary appeared to the three children on May 13, 1917. The apparitions continued once a month until October 13, 1917. When Francisco could not see Mary at first, Mary said Francisco should offer a rosary and he would see her. She also announced that Francisco and Jacinta would die soon, but that Lucia would live a long life. She added that Francisco "must say many rosaries."

Francisco was delighted at the news. From then on, he spent all his time saying the rosary and offering his prayers. He refused to go to school with Lucia. Instead, he walked to the village church to be with "the hidden Jesus." A quiet, gentle, serious boy,

Francisco prayed alone in front of the tabernacle. "I just want to comfort our Lord," he told his cousin.

During the many months of controversy over the apparitions, the three children were arrested and imprisoned. As they knelt on the stone floor, Francisco leading them in the rosary, other prisoners joined them. They survived the experience, and felt even greater peace because of the ordeal.

Sometimes, Francisco would disappear and his family would search for him only to find him "behind a little wall or a shrub, on his knees, praying," Lucia wrote later. When they asked why he did not invite them to pray with him, he answered, "Because I prefer to pray alone."

When Jacinta told people that Mary asked people to pray for sinners, Francisco corrected her. "We are not just to pray for sinners," he explained. "We are supposed to make sacrifices for sinners. We have been told to pray for world peace and an end to the war."

Francisco and Jacinta contracted the flu during the global influenza epidemic of the 1910s. Francisco died on April 4, 1919; Jacinta died a year later. Lucia died at age ninety-seven, on February 13, 2005, at the cloistered convent in Coimbra, Portugal. She spent her entire life, it was reported at the time of her death, praying for "reconciliation, conversion, and peace" for humanity.

I believe the Church missed one of the major points of the Fatima apparitions and enlisted it into the war on communism. Fatima called for an end to war itself. Ninety years later, the Cold War is over, communism has ended, and the Berlin Wall has fallen, yet the evils of war, capitalism, and nuclear weapons continue to kill and harm humanity, especially children and the poor. The message of Francisco and his friends calls for steadfast prayer for world peace and an end to war. If we take up this deliberate intention and live out its Gospel implications for peace in our daily lives, we will disarm, the world will disarm, nuclear weapons will be abolished, and war will finally be outlawed. Like the abolition of slavery, this seemingly impossible goal will become a reality. All we have to do is ask for the grace, for Christ's resurrection gift of peace.

Francisco, the child of peace, has become for me a teacher of peace. I want to take up where he left off, to continue that steadfast prayer for the abolition of war, and to storm heaven for a new world of nonviolence. Even in heaven, no doubt, Francisco continues to pray for the abolition of war.

Here in this icon, he prays for world peace and invites us to join him in that prayer:

God of peace,
Please help us end all the wars in the world right now.
Teach us never to wage war or risk war again.
Help us to beat our swords into plowshares,
to study war no more, and to love our enemies.
Give us the great gift of a new world
without war, violence, injustice, and nuclear weapons.
Make us your servants of peace.
Let us live in peace with all people everywhere,
that we may radiate your holy peace until that new day
when you welcome us into your house of peace. Amen.

21 | Miguel Pro
(1891-1927)

Miguel Pro was one of the best and brightest men the Society of Jesus ever produced. A bold, daring resister, he took on government oppression, and did so with wit and love as a disciple of Jesus. He was devoted to the cross, willing to give his life for the struggle of justice, and faced his inevitable execution in a spirit of peace, prayer, forgiveness, and gratitude.

Born on January 13, 1891, in Zacatecas, Mexico, Miguel was a happy, enthusiastic youth, ready with jokes and good cheer for any occasion. In 1910, he saw Halley's Comet fly by and cried out, "Just wait, littler stars, until you see how I shall outdo you by leaving my trail across the heavens!" He entered the Society of Jesus the following year, and spent the next few years studying and traveling through Texas, New Mexico, California, Spain, Nicaragua, and Belgium, where he was ordained a priest in 1925.

Miguel Pro suffered serious stomach problems all his life, and endured three unsuccessful operations. A few weeks after he returned to Mexico in 1926 for health reasons, the government closed all Catholic churches and started arresting priests. During this brutal anti-Catholic crackdown, he took up a secret ministry to Catholics. He resisted the government, supported the underground Church, and offered Mass and the sacraments to any

Catholics. He was able to get away with his underground work because he wore a variety of disguises. He posed as a chauffeur, a mechanic, a playboy, or a farm laborer. He even dressed up as a policeman, entered a jail, and heard confessions of Catholic prisoners awaiting execution. His biography reads like a Robert Ludlum thriller. It would make a great, holy, suspense film.

Miguel Pro tried to make people laugh. A practical joker, he once said that when he got to heaven and found it to be sad and serious, he would do a Mexican hat dance to cheer everybody up.

He was part of a Church movement that championed Christ—not the president or communism or Mexico—as the real Political Leader, our True King. Participants in the movement not only hid underground, but they also engaged in public actions to proclaim Christ's kingship. On one occasion, they released hundreds of balloons that dropped pro-Catholic leaflets.

After the Mexican president's life was threatened and the authorities discovered that the getaway car once belonged to one of Miguel's brothers, Miguel and his brothers were hunted down and arrested. After the president himself ordered the execution, reporters, politicians, and military leaders were brought in to witness the death of the trouble-making Jesuit. Miguel, however, did not know he was to be killed. On the morning of November 23, 1927, wearing a dark suit, with a vest, white shirt, and tie, he was brought outdoors to stand in front of a stone wall. Only then did he see the firing squad.

The authorities let Miguel have a moment to pray. Refusing the blindfold he was offered, he knelt down in silence and then stood up, held a rosary in one hand and his Jesuit vow crucifix in the other, and stretched out his arms in the form of a cross.

"May God have mercy on you," he said to his executioners. "May God bless you. Lord, you know that I am innocent. With all my heart, I forgive my enemies." Then just as his executioners were about to shoot, Miguel said in a firm, clear voice, *"Viva Christo Rey!"* ("Long live Christ the King!") Although the soldiers were shocked by his words, they started shooting, but failed to kill him. He fell backward, in the form of a cross, still alive. Then one of the soldiers walked over and shot him at close range, killing him instantly.

The photos of Miguel Pro's execution were distributed by the press throughout Mexico. But instead of stifling the resistance, as the government hoped, the visual images of Miguel's outstretched arms and his dead body fueled the Catholic resistance. Thousands marched at his funeral, and he was acclaimed a saint.

"If life be hard, love makes us stronger," Miguel Pro once wrote, "and only love, grounded on suffering, can carry the cross of Jesus." Like El Salvador's Jesuit martyr, Ignacio Ellacuría, Miguel Pro spoke of the cross and the kingship of Christ based on nonviolent suffering love. He understood that the cross comes through resistance to injustice, and that the duty of a disciple is to condemn injustice publicly. "You have to speak out against injustice," he said. "We must speak and cry out against injustice with confidence and not with fear."

Miguel believed in each person's call to leadership. "We should persuade ourselves with humility that we are the leaders in the name of the Church, not only in religious matters but also in social questions," he wrote. "We should widen our horizons, and look toward the future. We should not limit ourselves to a narrow ministry."

Throughout his persecution, Miguel Pro maintained a cheerful disposition and a deep faith that he was doing God's work and was destined for resurrection. "The most they can do is kill me," he said. "The splendor of the resurrection is already on its way because now the gloom of the passion is at its height."

In this icon, Miguel Pro holds a crown of thorns with a corporal, symbolizing his underground Masses. His shirt and tie resemble the clothes he wore when he was shot. The hand of Christ the King reaches down to give him an eternal crown. We too will be welcomed into the new life of resurrection, like Miguel, as we pursue the Gospel life of love and justice.

22 | Faustina Kowalska
(1905-1938)

Faustina of Poland resembles Bernadette of Lourdes. She was sent on a specific mission for the whole world, in this case, to be an apostle of Divine Mercy.

Helena Kowalska was born on August 25, 1905, in the village of Glogowiec, Poland. As a teenager, she wanted to enter religious life, but her parents would not let her. In 1924, she left for Warsaw, looking to join a convent. Because of her poor health, nearly every convent turned her down. Finally, the following year, the Sisters of Our Lady of Mercy accepted her. She entered the Order in August 1925 and took the name Mary Faustina, which means "Blessed One." Within months, she showed signs of the tuberculosis which would eventually kill her at age thirty-three.

On February 22, 1931, Sister Mary Faustina had a vision of Jesus. She saw him wearing white robes with one hand raised in blessing and the other on his heart, from which two rays issued downward, one red and one white. He told her to have a painting of the vision made, with a caption under it reading, "Jesus, I trust you." He also asked for a "Feast of Mercy" to be held on the first Sunday after Easter. Anyone who received the sacraments of the Eucharist and Reconciliation on that day would receive special mercy. "On that day the divine floodgates through which graces flow are opened," Jesus told her. "Let no soul fear to draw near to me, even though its sins be as scarlet. Humanity will not have peace until it turns to the fount of my mercy."

Even as Sister Mary Faustina sought out a painter, the visions continued. Three years later, in 1934, the painting finally was completed, although she was disappointed with it. April 28, 1935, was the first Feast of Divine Mercy. Sister Faustina died three years later, on October 5, 1938.

"This is the time of divine mercy," Jesus told Faustina. "Anyone who comes to me will have my mercy. I will shower the world with my mercy. My mercy is greater than all the grains of sand. But a time of judgment will also come."

When the painting was unveiled at a church in Vilnius, Faustina had another vision of Christ. This time, the two rays encompassed the entire world. She realized then that God's mercy reaches everyone, in every nation, in every corner of the world. Jesus wants us to receive his mercy, to live in his mercy, and to share his mercy with one another. He desires everyone to turn back to him, to be healed by his merciful touch, and then to reach out to everyone with that same holy mercy for the rest of our lives.

This unfathomable Divine Mercy is another way to understand the Gospel of nonviolence. Divine Mercy, like Gospel nonviolence, moves us to show boundless compassion toward everyone on the planet, beginning with our relatives and friends, to include our neighbors and communities, and finally, to spread even to strangers and enemies. Mercy transforms us. Once we feel the mercy of God, we can never again withhold mercy from

another. From that moment on, we forgive everyone who ever hurt us, and we grant clemency to oppressors and oppressed alike. Mercy leads us away from violence so that we live in peace with everyone. It pushes us to renounce war, revenge, retaliation, the death penalty, and nuclear weapons, so that all humanity might dwell in Divine Mercy.

If we truly honor Jesus as the image of Divine Mercy, support the Feast of Mercy after Easter, and study the life of St. Faustina, we will make the connections between the personal call to mercy and the global and political ramifications of divine mercy. We advocate mercy for the people of Iraq and Palestine, for those on death row as well as the unborn, for those who are different from us, for the hungry and the homeless, for people around the world regardless of race, creed, age, religion, or nationality. As we make these political connections and implement policies of mercy toward every human being on earth, especially toward those we do not believe are worthy of mercy, we begin to reflect the Divine Mercy of the Sacred Heart of Jesus. We understand how Jesus feels when he gives us the gift of divine mercy. Our participation in his mercy leads us to renewed gratitude for his kindness to us, the unmerciful.

"Jesus, grant that I may have love, compassion, and mercy for every soul without exception," Faustina prayed in her diary. "Jesus, each of your saints reflects one of your virtues. I desire to reflect your compassionate heart, full of mercy. I want to glorify it. Let your mercy, Jesus, be impressed upon my heart and soul like a seal." She knew the power of mercy to transform. "Jesus, make my heart like yours, or rather transform it into your own heart that I may sense the needs of other hearts, especially those who are sad and suffering," she prayed. "May the rays of mercy rest in my heart."

Thomas Merton defined God at the end of his journal, *The Sign of Jonas,* as "Mercy within Mercy within Mercy." In this icon, Faustina, the apostle of Divine Mercy, holds the painting of Jesus, inviting us into the light of Jesus' mercy. She inspires us to share that Divine Mercy with every person we meet for the rest of our lives. As people of Divine Mercy, we trust in Jesus and go forth to witness to his mercy by transforming the world from revenge, violence, and war into the light of his love, compassion, and peace.

23 | Josephine Bakhita
(1869-1947)

Josephine Bakhita was canonized on October 1, 2000, not just because of her heroic, saintly life, but because she symbolizes the plight of Africa itself. Her story is a story of resurrection and hope. Josephine was born in Darfur in 1869, present-day Sudan. In 1875, when she was six years old, she was kidnapped, sold into slavery, and throughout her youth was resold several times in the markets of El Obeid and Khartoum. Her owners tattooed her entire body, except her face, with a razor blade, and poured salt into her open wounds. During her torture, covered with blood, she begged for death. "I can truly say that it was a miracle I did not die," she later said, "because the Lord has destined me for greater things." Her name "Bakhita" was given to her by her kidnappers. It means "Fortunate One."

In 1883, Josephine was sold to Callisto Legnani, the Italian Consul, who treated her with kindness and intended to free her. In 1885, through his connections, she was taken to Italy. In 1888, she moved into the Catechumenate center run by the Daughters of Charity of Canossa, known as the Canossians, in Venice. In 1890, she was baptized and, three years later, entered the Canossian novitiate in Venice.

In the course of her healing, Josephine chose to forgive the people who kidnapped her. She took up the cause of children, and started to work at a school ministering to low-income children. She was known for her gentle presence, her friendly disposition, and her willingness to do any menial task to comfort suffering people. In 1930, a biography of her was published, and she became a much sought after speaker. During her talks, she raised funds to support the missions in Africa. She died in Schio, Italy, on February 8, 1947. She was a Canossian sister for over fifty years.

In 2004, Rev. Jesse Jackson called conditions in present-day Darfur, the birthplace of Josephine Bakhita, "the worst humanitarian catastrophe in the world." World media turned briefly to war-ravaged Darfar, where famine threatens four million people. Over 75,000 people died in Darfur between 2003 and 2005 from famine and violence due to the war between rebel groups and Sudanese militia. More than two million people in Darfur have been driven from their homes. In 2005, U.N. Secretary-General Kofi Anan called Darfur "hell on earth." Others have named it simply "genocide."

Today, Africa in general is devastated by AIDS, starvation, and war. It is crucified by first-world greed, neglect, apathy, violence, and injustice. Unless we demand massive economic, social, and medical aid for Africa, instead of military aid, unless we redistribute the world's resources equally to our African sisters and brothers, the catastrophe, the crucifixion of Africa, will continue.

More than 25 million Africans are currently infected with HIV. In March 2005, the United Nations issued a study that reported 80 million more Africans will die from AIDS by the year 2025. Infections could soar to 90 million, more than ten percent of the continent's population. The First World needs to spend $200 billion immediately to save 16 million people from death and 43 million people from becoming infected.

While there is no cure for HIV or AIDS, anti-retroviral drugs do help sufferers to live a normal life. But such drugs are too expensive for Africans, who live on less than a dollar a day and have no healthcare. Life expectancy in nine African countries has dropped to below forty. There are currently 11 million orphans because of AIDS, while 6,500 people die from the disease each day. While HIV/AIDS ravishes the continent, hunger continues to kill tens of thousands of Africans each month. According to Oxfam, a leading international relief organization, more than 842 million people suffer from hunger around the world. Thirty thousand children under the age of five die each day from hunger and preventable diseases related to hunger. Of the 6.2 billion people living in the world, more than a billion survive on less than $1 a day. Africa bears the brunt of hunger.

While hunger and HIV/AIDS devastate Africa, the United States is quietly militarizing Africa, as it has done in Latin America—this time with the intent of controlling Africa's rich oil reserves. The $200 billion spent on war in Iraq could have fed the masses in Darfur and provided free medicine to all HIV/AIDS sufferers in Africa. The legacy of colonialism, violence, racism, slavery, and injustice lives on, only in a different guise.

The heroic life of Josephine Bakhita offers a powerful witness on several fronts. First of all, she challenges first world racism and the legacy of colonialism and slavery that lives on in the crucifixion of our African sisters and brothers today. Her life demands that we renounce racism, create multi-cultural programs and institutions, and transform our divisive, racist culture into a culture of inclusivity and equality. She advocated for Africa until the end of her life, and she would want us to do the same, to demand food and medicine for sisters and brothers in Darfar and throughout the continent. She would lead the campaign to cancel Africa's debt and advocate fair trade. Her witness summons us to that great work.

Second, Josephine finds true healing only when she decides to forgive her kidnappers and torturers. Many might dismiss this act as simplistic or pious, but it is neither. It is brave, daring, and bold—the key to healing, inner peace, and personal transformation. Forgiveness is a deeply spiritual and political practice that has the power to heal and transform all of us. True healing comes only when we forgive those who hurt us, including those who physically assaulted and even tortured us. Josephine learned that if we want the forgiveness of God, we have to forgive everyone who ever hurts us. Indeed, her act of forgiveness opens new doors in her life by freeing her to reach out in loving service to others, as a follower of the forgiving Jesus. "If I were to meet the slave-traders who kidnapped me and even those who tortured me," she later said, "I would kneel and kiss their hands, for if that did not happen, I would not be a Christian."

Most of the world's problems, including most of the Church's problems, stem from our refusal to forgive. If we dare let go of our hurts, anger, bitterness, and resentment, if we forgive everyone who ever hurt us, we, too, will discover the contemplative depths of healing, and radiate a peace not of this world.

Finally, though she is a victim of brutal violence as a child, Josephine grows up to defend and advocate for impoverished children. She is known for her boundless compassion, especially for the vulnerable, powerless, and economically disenfranchised. That is the mark of sanctity.

"The Lord has loved me so much," she testified. "We, too, must love everyone. We must be compassionate to everyone." She would want us to advocate for the starving, suffering children of the world, especially in Africa.

The Canossian Sisters commissioned this icon in honor of Josephine's canonization. Here she stands, an African woman, holding the Christ Child and protecting children. She invites us to do the same, first, by standing in solidarity with the crucified children of Africa today, and working for a new day without hunger, war, or poverty.

· Hogar de Cristo ·

24 | Alberto Hurtado
(1905-1951)

Alberto Hurtado is not well known in North America, even though he was canonized in 2005. In Chile, however, he is the hero of the poor, a fighter for social justice, and a bright light of hope. He founded one of Chile's largest social organizations, *Hogar de Cristo,* which means, "House of Christ." Hurtado spent years walking the streets of Santiago, sheltering the homeless, feeding the hungry, and advocating for social justice on behalf of workers and poor people. As this icon shows, Alberto Hurtado became the "house of Christ." Without him, the poor, especially the homeless children of Chile, would have remained homeless.

Alberto Hurtado was born in Chile in 1905 and grew up in poverty. Throughout his life, he was known for his gentle, amiable, optimistic, and kind disposition. Because a neighborhood Jesuit school offered him a scholarship, he was educated by the Jesuits from first grade through college. He became active in the Church, eventually went to law school, and became an advocate for workers and labor unions.

In 1923, Alberto fulfilled his dream by entering the Jesuits. His studies took him to Argentina, Spain, Ireland, and eventually to Belgium, for theology degrees and ordination in 1933. He returned to Chile in 1934 and worked tirelessly on behalf of the poor and those in need until his death in 1951. He was dedicated, committed, selfless, and zealous. He taught at St. Ignatius School, gave countless retreats, wrote articles and books, and presided at Masses all over Santiago. He trained scores of young people in radical discipleship to Christ, urging them to ask themselves, "What would Christ do in my position?"

For Albert Hurtado, the poor were the focus of the Church, and the heart of the Gospel. "For the poor, the rich are nothing more than exploiters, fortunate beings, unworthy of their respect or consideration, devoid of any sentiments for the impoverished," he wrote while in Spain.

In 1941, he wrote a controversial and widely read book called, *Is Chile a Catholic Country?* He denounced Chile's growing secularization, urged the Church to side with laborers, unions, and the poor, and accused rich Catholics of rejecting church social teachings. He suffered constant criticism from all sides because many feared he was leading the Church into communism, but he also had the support of Jesuit officials and the Vatican.

That same year, Alberto became national director of Catholic Action, the international movement that mobilized thousands to work for the Church and those in need. He put in long days and the organization exploded. Young people responded eagerly to his call to work for "the reign of Christ in our midst." He published magazines, organized national conferences, and directed torchlight processions through Santiago. "If the times are bad," he would say, quoting St. Augustine, "then let us be better ourselves and the times will be better, for we are the times."

After a few years, he began to burn out and stepped down. Then one day, while preaching at morning Mass, he spoke about meeting a homeless man in the freezing rain the night before. He confessed that he did nothing to help the man and, as a result, could not sleep, fearing that Christ was present in that beggar. He said he would like to do something to help the poor, and so, after Mass, several women contributed money. One woman offered land for a building. That very day, Alberto went to the archbishop and received permission to start a new project for the poor. He wrote an article about it for the Santiago newspaper the next day, and overnight the program was launched. He called it "Hogar de Cristo." Its mission was "to give a roof to homeless beggars, food for their stomachs, education, and, if possible, work that would help them escape their terrible misery." Within weeks, he also opened two temporary homes: one for homeless boys and one for homeless women and children. Besides serving meals and providing clean places to sleep, he set up workshops that would help the homeless find work and change their lives.

"Christ stumbles through our streets in the person of so many poor who are hungry, thrown out of their miserable lodgings because of sickness and destitution," Alberto Hurtado wrote in one of his many fundraising appeals. "Christ has no home! And we who have the good fortune to have one and have food to satisfy our hunger, what are we doing about it?"

Hogar de Cristo touched a nerve, and money poured in, allowing for thousands to be housed and fed. Alberto was the first to name these desperate poor people as Christ in our midst. "I hold that every poor person, every vagrant, every beggar is

Christ carrying his cross. And as Christ, we must love and help them. We must treat them as our brothers and sisters, as human beings like ourselves." While he named the poor as Christ, he also insisted that the Gospel demands not just charity but justice. "Injustice causes infinitely more evil than charity could ever undo," he wrote. The ultimate task for the Church, he maintained, is to change the entire social system which forces thousands of human beings into misery.

At the time, Chile's political system turned thousands not only into the street poverty, but also what Alberto called "misery." Every night, he drove through Santiago in his famous green truck and picked up homeless people. He also wanted to get homeless youth permanently off the streets, so he founded an agricultural school in the countryside where any youth from Hogar de Cristo was welcome to study and work the land.

In his 1947 book, *Social Humanism,* Alberto Hurtado insisted that "there can be no fidelity to God without justice for human beings." True Christians cannot preach resignation to the poor, he wrote. They must lead the struggle for justice, and not just out of fear of communism but because the Gospel demands that we transform injustice into justice.

After traveling through the United States and Europe in 1947, Alberto Hurtado poured his energies into the labor union movement as director of the Association of Chilean Trade Union Action. Because he defended workers rights and labor unions, he suffered countless attacks from all sides, but he persisted because he knew that Catholic social teaching insists on justice for workers. Despite the criticism, his movement blossomed within a few short years.

By 1949, Hogar de Cristo sheltered over 141,000 people and distributed 373,000 meals. Alberto bought a new building to house the administration of both Hogar de Cristo and the labor association. When the board of directors met, he still needed to raise another one million pesos. As a result, the board refused to support his project. Just at that moment, however, a woman knocked at the door and offered a contribution. He thanked her, as usual, since people offered contributions to him wherever he went. But when he opened the note during the meeting, he discovered one million pesos. His project moved ahead.

In those last years, Alberto Hurtado started a national Catholic magazine, *Mensaje;* published several more books and articles; gave a series of talks on national radio; and founded a lay fraternity vowed to serve Christ in the poor. By 1951, Hogar de Cristo had sheltered 700,000 homeless people and served some 1,800,000 meals to the poor.

On May 19, 1951, Alberto Hurtado was diagnosed with pancreatic cancer. He suffered terribly, but never complained. He died at peace on August 18, 1951. Throughout his life, he maintained a simple motto, *"Contento, Señor, contento,"* "Happy, my Lord. I'm happy." He was happy knowing that every day he served Christ in the poor, defended Christ in the poor, and offered a home to Christ in the homeless. He prays that we will carry on that great legacy.

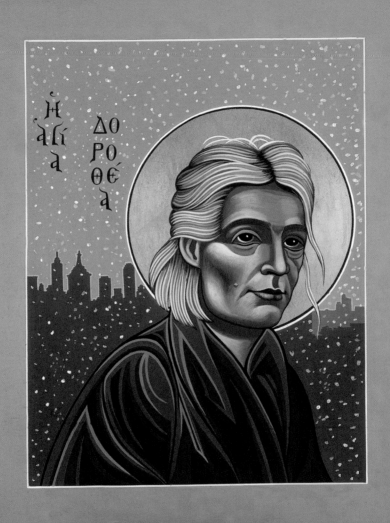

25 | Dorothy Day

(1897-1980)

Dorothy Day was born in Chicago on November 8, 1897. As a radical activist and journalist living in New York City's Greenwich Village, she fought for labor rights, women's rights, and an end to World War I. In 1927, after her daughter Tamar was born, she was filled with gratitude and received the gift of faith. She decided that the two of them should be baptized in the Church. In response, her partner promptly left her.

It was 1932, and Dorothy didn't know what to do or how to be a radical Catholic Christian. While attending a march against hunger in Washington, D.C., she prayed that God would open up a way for her to practice her radical politics as a devout Catholic. Her prayer was answered in the person of Peter Maurin, a French peasant intellectual who was waiting for her back in New York. Within a few months, they founded the Catholic Worker Movement. Seventy-five years later, the Catholic Worker still runs over 140 houses of hospitality for the homeless, publishes many newspapers, and manages a few farming communes.

For the rest of her life, until her death on November 29, 1980, Dorothy Day was the single most important voice on behalf of the Gospel of peace and justice in the North American

Church. "Poverty is my vocation," she once said, "to live as simply and as poorly as I can and never to cease talking and writing of poverty and destitution." In her book *Loaves and Fishes,* she wrote: "I condemn poverty and I advocate it. Anything you do not need belongs to the poor . . . Once we begin not to worry about what kind of house we are living in, what kind of clothes we are wearing, once we give up the stupid recreation of the world, we have time which is priceless—to remember that we are all our brothers' and sisters' keepers and that we must not only care for their needs as far as we are immediately able, but we must try to build a better world."

Robert Coles tells a classic story about his first visit with Dorothy Day in 1952. He entered the ramshackle Catholic Worker house on Mott Street in New York City to find the main room filled with tables and a large messy kitchen. Two people sat at one of the tables, one of them was Dorothy Day, the other was a drunk woman with a large, purple-red birthmark on her face who talked on and on nonsensically. All the while, Dorothy sat right there, listening intently, as Coles relates:

> When would it end—the alcoholic ranting and the silent nodding, occasionally interrupted by a brief question, which only served, maddeningly, to wind up the already over talkative one rather than wind her down? Finally, silence fell upon the room. Dorothy Day asked the woman if she would mind an interruption. She got up and came over to me. She said, "Are you waiting to talk with one of us?" One of us: with those three words she cut through layers of self-importance, a lifetime of bour-

geois privilege, and scraped the hard bone of pride. With those three words, so quietly and politely spoken, she had indirectly told me what the Catholic Worker Movement is all about and what she herself was like.

What made Dorothy Day a living saint, however, was not just her extraordinary charity work for the poor, but her determination to find the causes of poverty and change the system that leaves billions of people impoverished, which crucifies Christ all over again. She made the connection among poverty, injustice, and war. She demanded not only charity for the poor, but justice as well. She knew that the billions of dollars that should be spent on food, homes, healthcare, education, and jobs for the poor were spent instead on war and weapons. She realized that war not only made people poor and hungry, it killed them. Therefore she advocated the works of mercy, and also the works of peace and justice.

In her solidarity with the poor, she stood up to defend them against the evils of war, weapons, and injustice. She was arrested repeatedly throughout her life for civil disobedience against war and injustice. She even said that we can measure our discipleship only by how much trouble we are in for our stand for peace and justice. In the late 1950s, she joined a small group in New York City that refused to go underground during mandatory air-raid drills in preparation for a nuclear attack. Each year, the group repeated their civil disobedience and spent a month in prison. Then, in 1961, when 2,000 people refused to go underground, the air-raid drills were stopped. She supported those who resisted the Vietnam War, and famously proposed that the best resistance was to "fill the jails!" By 1972, at age seventy-five, she was arrested in California for protesting with Cesar Chavez on behalf of exploited farm workers.

"All our talks about peace and the weapons of the Spirit are meaningless," she wrote, "unless we try in every way to embrace voluntary poverty and not work in any position, any job, that contributes to war, not to take any job whose pay comes from the fear of war, or the atomic bomb."

Dorothy consistently denounced every war during her lifetime, at a time when no other Catholic was even questioning the idea of war. She publicly denounced both World Wars, the Korean War, the Vietnam War, and the U.S. wars in Central America. Instead, she upheld the unpopular, widely ignored Gospel mandate that we love our enemies, serve the poor, feed the hungry, house the homeless, and welcome Christ in the stranger. She advocated voluntary poverty, radical nonviolence, personalism, direct service of those in need, and public witnessing on behalf of the Gospel. Almost single-handedly she broke new ground for the Church. Her influence is far greater than we can measure.

"As we come to know the seriousness of the situation—the wars, the racism, the poverty, the nuclear weapons," Dorothy Day once wrote, "we come to realize that things will not be changed simply by words or demonstrations. Rather it's a question of living one's life in a drastically different way."

"Becoming a saint is the revolution," Dorothy wrote. As the Church proceeds to canonize her, the rest of us need to take up her challenge and become saints like her—by serving Christ in the poor, resisting war, and advocating Christ's reign of peace.

This stunning icon is based on a photo of Dorothy Day when she was in her thirties. She looks at us, questioning the way we love, inviting us to join her Gospel experiment, and summoning us to the holiness of voluntary poverty and creative nonviolence.

"All my prayers, my own suffering, my reading, my study would lead me to this conclusion, that love is a great and holy force and must be used as a spiritual weapon," she wrote. "Love against hate. Suffering against violence. What is two thousand years in the history of the world? We have scarcely begun to love. We have scarcely begun to know Christ, to see him in others around us."

In *Loaves and Fishes,* she names our challenge: "The greatest challenge of the day is: how to bring about a revolution of the heart, a revolution which has to start with each one of us. When we begin to take the lowest place, to wash the feet of others, to love our brothers and sisters with that burning love, that passion, which led to the cross, then we can truly say, 'Now I have begun.'"

26 | Jean Donovan
(1953-1980)

I remember exactly where I was when I heard the news that four U.S. churchwomen were raped and killed in El Salvador on December 2, 1980. I was a senior at Duke University, with plans to enter the Jesuits the following year. But I was having second thoughts. What difference could I make? How can one witness to Christ in such a harsh world? Why bother?

When I bent down to pick up the *Durham Morning Herald*, I saw the headline: "Four Churchwomen Killed in El Salvador." The bodies of Sisters Ita Ford, Maura Clarke, and Dorothy Kazel, and lay missioner Jean Donovan were found in a shallow grave in a barren countryside not far from the San Salvador airport.

The witness of the deaths of these four women changed my life; I reconfirmed my decision to become a Jesuit. Within a few years, I befriended Jean's parents, Pat and Ray Donovan, and organized speaking events for them around the country. In 1985, while living and working in El Salvador, I traveled into the countryside to pray at the lonely deserted place where they were killed. A stone cross marks the spot, and a plaque there reads: "Ita Ford, Maura Clarke, Dorothy Kazel, and Jean Donovan gave their lives on December 2, 1980. Receive them, Lord, into your kingdom."

Jean Donovan, along with the heroic sisters, offers a rare

Gospel witness in these brutal times. Jean was born on April 10, 1953, and grew up in upper-middle-class Westport, Connecticut. She attended Mary Washington College in Virginia, and spent a life-changing year in Ireland, where a charismatic priest committed to the Latin American poor challenged her not to waste her life pursuing money but rather, to give her life pursuing God and serving God's poor. In late 1977, Jean quit her executive position at the Cleveland, Ohio, branch of Arthur Andersen, a national accounting firm, turned her back on frst-world North America, gave away her Harley Davidson, said goodbye to friends, and joined the Maryknoll Lay Mission program to follow Jesus among the third-world poor in El Salvador.

After an orientation at Maryknoll in New York and Spanish studies in Guatemala, Jean was assigned to the Cleveland Mission Program in a poor parish in La Libertad, El Salvador, near the ocean. For the next few years, she served the parish, managed its budget, played with the children, and helped other Church workers. But the brutal government's war against the poor intensified. The streets were filled with soldiers, and dead bodies were left along the roads. Jean and the sisters began to pick up the bodies and bury them. Then they turned their attentions to supporting the distraught relatives who searched for their "disappeared" loved ones.

Jean and the rest of El Salvador found hope in the fearless homilies of Archbishop Oscar Romero. She wrote to a friend that his message was convincing her that prayer does make a difference. In gratitude, she baked a batch of chocolate chip cookies and delivered them to Archbishop Romero every Sunday afternoon after his morning Mass.

On March 24, 1980, Romero was shot while presiding at an evening Mass. Grieving deeply, Jean stood next to his coffin during the all-night wake. During the funeral Mass, the government threw bombs into the crowd of 30,000 mourners, killing 30. Although Jean was terrified, she told herself that if she was killed, she would go straight to God.

"I got your letter," Jean wrote to a friend afterwards, "and I really appreciate the fact that you said you worry about me. It's nice to know that people care and they'd like to tell me to come home, as you say. There are lots of times I feel like coming home. But I really do feel strongly that God has sent me here, and wants me to be here, and I'm going to try to do my best to live up to that."

Jean stayed in touch with her Irish priest friend. "Things now are so much worse, it's unbelievable," she wrote him in May 1980. "People are being killed daily. We just found out that three people from our area had been taken, tortured, and hacked to death. Two were young men and one was an older man. The man had been in a government death squad, had a fight with them and quit. So that's probably why they got him. We had done a mission out there recently and they were coming to the celebrations. Everything is really hitting so close now." That summer, Jean's two closest friends were assassinated after they took her to a movie and walked her home. Their violent deaths devastated her.

In September, Jean took a six-week vacation. First, she flew to Miami to see her parents, then to London to meet her boyfriend, then to Ireland for the wedding of a friend, then to Maryknoll in New York, then to Cleveland and Miami again.

A friend from Maryknoll later told Jean's parents that she spent several hours in the Maryknoll chapel. She confessed her fear that she might be killed. "She went into the chapel," Pat Donovan recalled, "and Jean was a great one for talking with God, and if she got answers, she's the only one that heard them, but when she came out two hours later, the sister said that she was an entirely different woman. She was ready to go back. She had somehow reconciled herself to what was happening and what she was to do, and she had made her peace with whatever frightening thoughts she had. She was really the old Jeannie when we put her back on the plane, joking, laughing."

Back in El Salvador, Jean started again to pick up the bodies, console the grieving, and lead the poor in prayer. "The Peace Corps left today and my heart sank low," she wrote a friend. "The danger is extreme and they were right to leave . . . Now I must assess my own position, because I am not up for suicide. Several times I have decided to leave El Salvador. I almost could, except for the children, the poor, bruised victims of this insanity. Who would care for them? Whose heart could be so staunch as to favor the reasonable thing in a sea of their tears and loneliness? Not mine, dear friend, not mine."

A few weeks before her death, she wrote of her efforts and her spiritual journey. "The situation is bad and believe it or not, at times I'm actually helpful. I also was trying to deal with some close friends who had been killed the last week of August. We are still plugging along. Life continues with many interruptions. I don't know how the poor survive. People in our positions really have to die to ourselves and our wealth to gain the spirituality of the poor and oppressed. I have a long way to go on that score.

They can teach you so much with their patience and their wanting eyes. We are all so inadequate in our help. I am trying now more and more to deal with the social sin of the First World."

Sometime that November, while riding her motorbike through the countryside, Jean noticed that a U.S. military helicopter was following her. When she later told the U.S. ambassador about it, he denied that U.S. helicopters were in El Salvador, and asked how she could tell. She told him that her father spent his life helping to build them, so she knew the name and model, much to the ambassador's chagrin.

On the evening of December 2, Jean and Dorothy drove to the airport to meet Ita and Maura, who were returning from Managua. The four women were last seen alive driving from the airport down the main road. Two days later, their bodies were discovered in a makeshift grave about fifteen miles away. They had been raped and shot at close range. Jean's face was completely destroyed. She was twenty-seven years old.

Jean Donovan and the other churchwomen invite us to enter the world of the poor, to share their powerlessness and pain, and to risk the consequences of this Christian solidarity. Jean challenges us to defend the poor, stay with the poor, even give our lives for the poor, as Jesus did. Her witness summons us to do whatever we can to help the poor, to walk with the poor, to stand with the poor, to speak up for the poor, and to become, like Jesus on the cross, one with the poor.

In the face of the poor, the broken, battered, bruised, beaten people of Central America; in the face of the refugees, the homeless, the hungry, the sick, and the displaced; yes, even in the face of the enemy; Jean Donovan saw the face of Christ. In the midst of the poor, she discovered not only the meaning of life, but also the presence of the living God. After such a spiritual encounter, there could be no turning back. As Jean entered the world of the poor and responded with compassionate love, the unarmed Christ disarmed Jean and gave her his spirit of nonviolent love, which empowered her to stand with the powerless even unto death. In the end, she knew a peace not of this world.

After her daughter's death, Pat Donovan found a prayer that Jean had written and left in her Bible. It read simply: "I pray that I will be an example of Christ's love and peace. I pray that people will always be more important to me than the job I do." Jean's prayer came true. As she looks out at us through this beautiful icon, she holds up the cross and prays with us that we, too, will exemplify Christ's love and peace by serving the poor and giving our lives for them—as she did.

27 | Hans Urs von Balthasar
(1905-1988)

Anyone who believes in God and thinks about God is, by definition, a theologian, for theology is simply the study of God. As everyday theologians, we can ask ourselves: What is God like? What is our image of God? How do we reflect the nature of God? How does Jesus reveal the mystery of God?

The last century saw an array of luminous theologians. Hans Urs von Balthasar is considered one of the greatest. He wrote on every aspect of Christian life and continues to inspire reflection on the meaning of life and the mystery of God.

Hans von Balthasar was born on August 12, 1905, in Lucerne, Switzerland. After studying at the universities of Vienna, Berlin, and Zurich, he completed his doctorate at Zurich in 1929. After making the thirty-day silent retreat of St. Ignatius Loyola, von Balthasar entered the Jesuits on November 18, 1928. He continued his Jesuit studies in Munich, Lyons, and Basel. In 1936, he was ordained a priest.

In the following years, von Balthasar published his main work—fifteen volumes in three parts called *The Glory of the Lord, Theo-Drama,* and *Theo-Logic.* He wrote on Christ, scripture, and love. *The Glory of the Lord* speaks of beauty as one of the ultimate manifestations of God. In fact, he called God

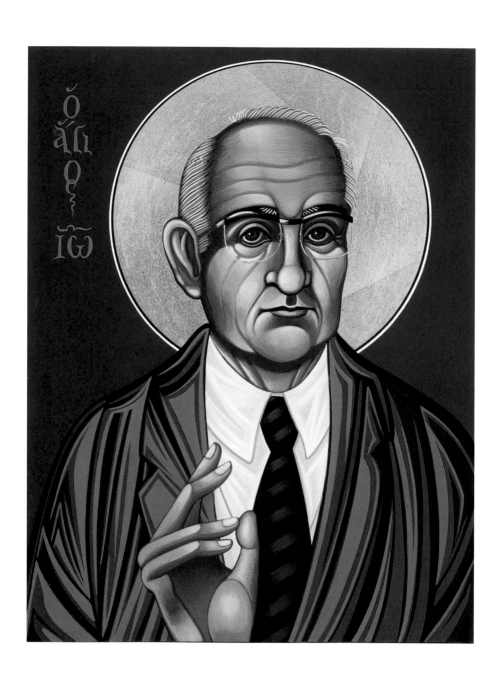

"Beauty." He also wrote about the saints, calling them lovers who "teach us the way to God." He wrote that "lovers are the ones who know most about God, and the theologian must listen to them." For von Balthasar, the point of life is to search for God and to know God. His groundbreaking book, *Prayer,* explained that prayer is ultimately the experience of our relationship with God, so we have no need to fear when we pray.

"The deepest thing in Christianity is God's love for the earth," von Balthasar wrote. "That God is rich in his heaven is something known also by other religions. That he wanted to be poor together with his creatures, that in his heaven, he wanted to and did indeed suffer for his world, and that through his Incarnation he enabled himself to prove his love to his creatures: this is the hitherto unheard-of thing."

Von Balthasar was a close friend of the great Protestant theologian Karl Barth, but his greatest colleague was a Swiss doctor, Adrienne von Speyr, who was born on 1902 and died in 1967. He called her one of the greatest mystics and theologians of our time. By the time of his death, he had edited sixty volumes of her writings. Together, they founded the Community of St. John, which he served as spiritual director. In 1951, when the Society of Jesus challenged his support of von Speyr and the Community of St. John, he decided to leave the Jesuits.

Leaving the Jesuits was the greatest crisis in von Balthasar's life. He was devoted to the Society of Jesus, but his superiors were cruel to him and his work was misunderstood. He discerned that God wanted him to continue his theological work with von Speyr and the Community of St. John, despite the objections of Jesuit superiors. He supported himself by giving speeches throughout Europe until six years later, when a bishop accepted him as a diocesan priest. But the controversy continued. He was not allowed to teach in any Catholic university or to attend the Second Vatican Council. Still he continued to write, translate, and publish, and, in the early 1970s, started his own publishing house. After von Speyr's death, he published dozens of her books. He also founded *Communio,* an international theological journal.

In the 1980s, Pope John Paul II asked von Balthasar to serve as his theologian, and to give workshops and retreats for him and the Curia. Over the years, von Balthasar asked John Paul II to apologize for the sins of the Church, including the Crusades, the Inquisition, violence against women and indigenous peoples, and Catholic support for Nazi genocide, an act which the pope did shortly before the millennium. Von Balthasar also urged the pope to abolish the office of cardinal. Von Balthasar wrote an open letter to Opus Dei, pointing out that their secrecy betrays the Gospel of Jesus. The pope responded by naming him a cardinal. On June 26, 1988, as he was preparing to preside at Mass, just two days before he was to made a cardinal, von Balthasar suddenly died of a heart attack.

In this icon, von Balthasar blesses us and invites us to become theologians. He calls us to reflect on the meaning of our lives, the mystery of God, and the presence of God in our lives. If we become everyday theologians, thinking constantly about God, we, too, will grow in love for God and witness to God's loving presence in the world.

28 | A. T. Thomas
(1951-1997)

On October 27, 1997, the decapitated body of a forty-six-year-old Jesuit priest was found in the countryside of India. His death was hardly noticed in the U.S. media or the Church, but his life and witness rank him alongside of John the Baptist and John de Britto, martyrs who were also beheaded for their witness to the Gospel of Jesus. A. T. Thomas is the model Jesuit, even a model Christian, because he showed the greatest love possible by laying down his life for the poor.

As a young Jesuit, A. T. Thomas, whose formal name was Thomas Anchanikal, decided that he would spend his life in loving service of the poor. After he was ordained in 1981, he worked in a parish, but dedicated his time to the dalits, the lowest Indian caste formerly known as "untouchables." He lived and worked among hungry, homeless dalits in Hazaribag, in Bihar state, India. Bihar has over 88 million people, at least a third of them illiterate, all of them impoverished. Making their plight his own, he became their advocate and defender. He opened schools, held community forums, and pushed for their civil rights. He wanted every dalit child to attend school, although most do not go to school, but instead look for ways to make money for their families. A. T. and his colleagues started night schools to teach every-

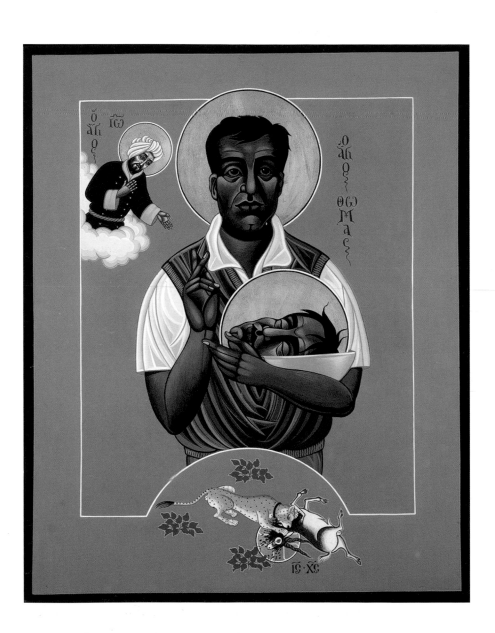

one how to read and write. In the process, he spent long hours listening to their stories of oppression and injustice.

In a 1993 film interview, A. T. Thomas spoke eloquently about his work among the poor. His manner is gentle, humble, and compassionate, but as he speaks, his steadfast, selfless dedication to the poor comes through. Instead of speaking of the lowest caste as untouchables or dalits, he uses the name Gandhi gave to them: Harijans, or Children of God. "We try to be with them," he explains, "and when we are with them, things happen. Being extremely poor, they are on the receiving end of society. I try to unite them, to help them stand up for their rights, to help them come to the realization that they are human beings. This involves education, healthcare, and women's programs, and so, lots of community-building sessions and informal meetings. We try to build a sense of unity and community and oneness. Our work appears to be political, but it is not along political lines. It is simply the work of the Gospel. Like Jesus, we are trying to be one with the people."

A. T. Thomas explains the conditions in India: "India is a violent country, with much institutionalized violence, with many killings and atrocities against the harridans. The vast majority of people have no voice. They cannot speak out for their rights. In Bihar, the violence is aimed at the poor. They are gunned down. Their houses are burned down. They are demoralized in a hundred and one ways."

When asked if he was afraid about being killed for his solidarity with the dalits, A. T. responds by saying this is a real possibility. "My Jesuit provincial just asked me about that yesterday!" he answers. "Yes, it is a possibility, I told him. But when one works for the poor, these are the things which one has to face. Jesus would not have died on the cross if he had not made the option for the poor. He would have died from a heart attack. Jesus made the option for the poor and he inspires me to do the same."

In 1996, A. T. moved to Manila to earn a master's degree in sociology. He hoped that this degree would give him the credentials and tools to better serve the dalits. In October 1997, he went back to India to visit friends and to do research for his degree. A few years earlier, he had led a legal fight against the mafia-type, upper-caste landlords who stole the dalits' land for their higher caste. A. T. hired lawyers and brought the landlords to court, and much to everyone's surprise, won. The landlords' thugs were sent off to prison, but they never forgot that their imprisonment was due to this troublemaking Jesuit. On October 24, 1997, A. T. visited a school he had built with another priest for the dalits, then stopped by the village of Sirka to visit friends. When he came upon some people dressed as police officers, beating one of the dalits, he immediately told them to stop the violence. One of the bullies recognized A. T. as the Jesuit who sent him to prison. The others surrounded him and led him away at gunpoint. The dalits objected, but it was too late. Two days later, his body was found in a river bed. He had been tortured and beaten, then decapitated. His hands were tied and many of his bones were broken.

In this shocking icon, Bill McNichols draws upon the ancient tradition that portrays John the Baptist as a risen martyr who holds his head on a plate. In the upper left-hand corner, we see John de Britto, another Jesuit martyr, honoring A. T. Thomas.

John de Britto was a Portuguese Jesuit priest who was beheaded in India in 1693 for trying to evangelize a ruling prince. Now he welcomes A. T. Thomas, his successor, into heaven. The icon is disturbing, as it should be. The brutal deaths of John the Baptist, Jesus, John de Britto, and A. T. Thomas should wake us from our complacency and push us into the struggle for justice.

If Christians are to reclaim the story of John the Baptist and Jesus, not only do we have to give our lives to that struggle for justice for the poor, but we, too, must risk them, as A. T. did, so that the poor will have justice and an authentic Gospel witness for Jesus will be proclaimed. That means we too must stand with the Children of God. We must touch "the untouchables," and pay the price of reaching out to our sisters and brothers in love.

detail

29 | Mychal Judge
(1933-2001)

On the morning of September 11, 2001, I was having breakfast with my parents at their hotel in Manhattan when we heard that a plane had crashed into the World Trade Center Towers. My parents left town before both buildings collapsed, and I went downtown to St. Vincent's Hospital to try to help. In two days, Red Cross officials asked me to help coordinate chaplains at the main Family Assistance Center. I worked there full-time for three months with over 500 chaplains of all religions, and counseled some 1,500 relatives and 500 firefighters and rescue workers at Ground Zero. All the while, I marched and organized demonstrations against the U.S. bombing raids on Afghanistan.

After leaving Ground Zero on Friday afternoon September 14, I stopped by the Church of St. Francis of Assisi on West Thirty-First Street, near Madison Square Garden, to attend the wake of Franciscan Father Mychal Judge, the chaplain of the New York Fire Department, one of the first New Yorkers killed that terrible morning.

The lower church was only half full. As I knelt at his closed casket, I felt a wave of grace and consolation come upon me. I thanked him for his life, and prayed for his blessing upon my life, my work with the grieving families, and my work in the peace movement. The next day, over 3,000 people attended his funeral, which was broadcast live around the world. He was hailed as a real hero.

Mychal Judge was born in Brooklyn on May 11, 1933, entered the Franciscans in 1954, and was ordained in 1961. He then served as pastor of two New Jersey parishes. During the 1980s, he ministered to those dying of AIDS and to alcoholics. In 1986, he was assigned to St. Francis of Assisi Church in Manhattan, and, in 1992, he was named chaplain to the New York City Fire Department. "I always wanted to be a priest or a fireman," he said at the time. "Now I'm both!" Within a short time, he gained the respect of every firefighter in New York City.

Mychal Judge was exceptionally outgoing, friendly, open, and extroverted. Another Franciscan recalled later that he "treated everyone like family." He regularly talked to thousands of people from parishioners, the ill, firefighters, or other Franciscans. In 1996, when TWA flight 800 crashed off Long Island killing 230 people, Mychal spent long days consoling distraught relatives.

About a month before he died, Mychal Judge had a strong sense from his prayer that his life would soon end, and so he decided to give away his few possessions. A friend of his, who is also a friend of mine, received a box full of his books. Then, when word came that a plane had crashed into one of the World Trade Center Towers on the morning of September 11, Mychal immediately went downtown with other firemen. Mayor Giuliani saw him rush by with several firemen and grabbed him by the arm. "Mychal, please pray for us," he said. "I always do!"

Mychal responded with a nervous smile.

A few months after the catastrophe, a documentary on national television showed footage of the lobby area inside the first tower only minutes before it collapsed. Father Mychal Judge is seen walking by slowly, looking distressed and worried, his hand and lips moving slowly. Many presume he was saying the rosary. Moments later, he went outside to bless the bodies of a firefighter and a woman. Just as he removed his helmet, steel debris fell on him, striking him in the back of the head, killing him instantly. The photograph of firefighters carrying his dead body minutes later to nearby St. Peter's Church traveled around the world. Father Mychal Judge was sixty-eight years old.

During the weeks after September 11, I met hundreds of firefighters at Ground Zero and the Family Assistance Center. On several occasions, I came upon a circle of ten or twenty firefighters, standing together in silence, in a state of shock. I did not know what to say to them, so I would ask them about Father Mychal Judge. Immediately, their faces would light up. They always knew him. More than once, I was told about how he would enter a hall during some firefighters banquet and announce in a loud voice, "You are all doing God's work, therefore, all your sins are forgiven!" He routinely gave this general absolution. When the cardinal of New York heard about it, however, Mychal was called in, reprimanded, and told never to do it again. But he disobeyed and continued to offer firefighters the mercy of God's forgiveness. Many of them told me how grateful they were.

"Father Mychal was the kindest guy in the world," a fire captain said afterwards. "He always had time for everyone." Mychal told my friend that when he got up in the morning, he allowed himself two minutes for "a pity party—to feel sorry for myself." After that, he went to work, helping and serving those in need, whomever he met.

Father Mychal Judge was a friend of Father Bill McNichols. In 1986, he showed up at one of Bill's monthly healing Masses for people with AIDS, asking how he could help. After September 11, Bill recalled an ancient icon entitled "The Protecting Veil of the Mother of God," which shows Mary holding out her veil to gather those crying out to her. In this icon, Mychal Judge holds out the protecting veil to receive the souls from the World Trade Center attacks. Saint Francis stands behind him, showing his wounds, guiding him, praying with him.

Like Francis, Mychal Judge gave his life in loving kindness, selfless service, and steadfast compassion. He is a witness to Gospel love, to the greatest love of all—laying down our lives in love for others.

"Lord, take me where you want me to go," Mychal Judge said in a prayer he once wrote. "Let me meet who you want me to meet. Tell me what you want me to say, and keep me out of your way."

30 | Philip Berrigan
(1923-2002)

"Those who truly believe in nonviolence, in justice, have no choice but to break unjust laws," Philip Berrigan wrote in his autobiography, *Fighting the Lamb's War.* He spent his life breaking unjust laws, protesting war, dismantling nuclear weapons, and spending years in prison for his Gospel peacemaking. One of the towering figures in recent Christian history, he was a true prophet, like Jeremiah or Ezekiel, sent by God to speak God's word of peace and disarmament. He denounced the empire's wars and weapons, and announced God's reign of peace and nonviolence, the most unpopular but most crucial truth of our time: that if we do not disarm our nuclear arsenal and abolish war, we are doomed to our own self-destruction. His steadfast witness for Christ's peace gave courage to thousands, led to countless demonstrations for disarmament, and may have helped prevent the further use of nuclear weapons.

Philip Berrigan was born on October 5, 1923, the youngest of six boys born to Thomas and Frida Berrigan. His brother Daniel, two years older, entered the Jesuits in 1939. Phil, instead, joined the army and picked targets for bombing raids during World War II. Afterwards, he enrolled at Holy Cross College and then entered the Josephites. After being ordained a Catholic priest in 1955, he spent years serving low-income African-

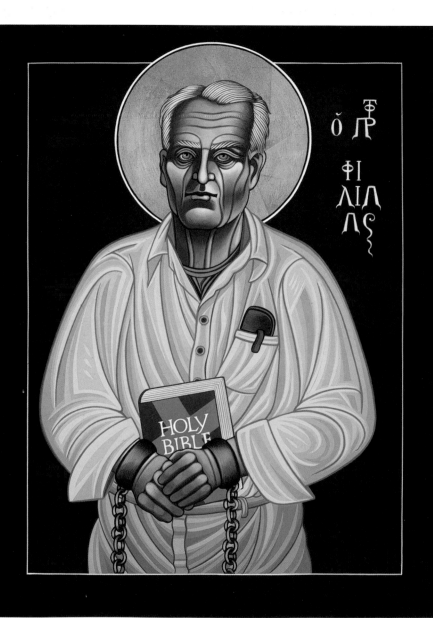

Americans in New Orleans, marching for civil rights, supporting the Freedom Riders, and condemning racism.

During the Cuban Missile Crisis, Philip began to make the connections among racism, poverty, war, and nuclear weapons. With the help of his brother Daniel, John Heidbrink, and the Fellowship of Reconciliation, Philip rethought his support of American militarism. By the time he moved to Newburgh, New York, in 1964, he and his brother were speaking out against the Vietnam War. He lobbied, wrote, and even protested at the home of the Secretary of Defense in Washington, D.C. This unusual activism cost him. He was transferred to Baltimore, Maryland.

As the war worsened, Philip's resistance deepened. On October 3, 1967, he and three friends poured blood on draft files, were arrested, and faced six years in prison. This protest, known as the Baltimore Four, drew enormous publicity. But when released on bond, Phil set to work organizing an even bigger nonviolent raid. On May 17, 1968, the Catonsville Nine, including Philip and his brother Daniel, poured homemade napalm on hundreds of draft files outside of Baltimore. The action shocked the nation, especially the image of two priest brothers breaking the law. That fall, they were found guilty, and later served several years in Danbury prison.

"Jail for me was an entirely voluntary affair, one of the predictable consequences connected with serious political dissent," Philip said. "This is not to say that I chose jail, or preferred it, but only that I felt civil disobedience was a Christian duty, and accepted jail as a consequence."

After his release from prison, Phil left the priesthood and married Elizabeth McAlister. Together, in 1973, they founded Jonah House, a community of nonviolent resistance in Baltimore. For the rest of his life, he organized demonstrations against the Vietnam War, nuclear weapons, and the industry of war in general. On September 9, 1980, with his brother Daniel and the Plowshares Eight, he entered a G.E. nuclear weapons plant in King of Prussia, Pennsylvania, where he hammered on an unarmed Mark 12A nuclear nosecone to "beat swords into plowshares." He later participated in three other Plowshares actions.

I first met Phil Berrigan in December 1982 in a Washington, D.C., church basement where a small group was preparing a vigil and nonviolent action at the Pentagon. Phil was a tall, imposing man with white hair, blue eyes, a big smile, and a commanding presence. I knew him for twenty years, and demonstrated against war with him on countless occasions.

On December 7, 1993, Philip, Bruce Friedrich, Lynn Fredriksson, and I walked illegally onto the Seymour Johnson Air Force Base near Goldsboro, North Carolina, where we hammered on a F15E nuclear-capable fighter bomber. Phil, Bruce, and I spent eight months together in a tiny county jail cell. Once I found a sheet of paper on his bunk with a long list of names on it, from "Prince of Peace" to "Wonder Counselor" to "Holy Wisdom." I asked about it, and he told me he was reciting these names for God as a mantra, as a way to pray. He showed the most single-minded commitment against nuclear weapons that I have witnessed.

"The bomb makes every other issue redundant," Phil told me when I interviewed him in 1992 for a peace journal.

The fact that we are complicit in the presence of the bomb—because we help pay for it, we allow its deployment and possible use, and we have threatened to use it at least 25 times unilaterally during the last 47 years of the Cold War—

destroys us spiritually, morally, psychologically, emotionally, and humanly. Our complicity in the bomb makes us incapable of dealing with lesser social and political problems that are in reality spin-offs of our dedication to the bomb.

The only conversion that is real today is a conversion that accepts responsibility for the bomb. This conversion turns one's life around so that one is free enough to witness against this inhuman, incredibly wicked manifestation of our insanity. We all have to take responsibility for the bomb. This conversion and responsibility will breed all sorts of life-giving, salvific benefits. It will create a just social order.

You can't maintain a superpower status unless you're armed to the teeth. So the U.S. will continue with weapons development, Star Wars, and a permanent war economy, because to do otherwise is to shift the status quo and redistribute wealth. The last people who want to do that are the one/two-hundredth who control thirty-seven percent of what the country produces, and their representatives, the president and his official terrorists in Washington. We need to resist this business of making war. We're called to serve the poor, resist the state and be ignored, ostracized and sent to jail because we do that.

Today, we are condemned to being hostages of the bomb. Legally, we've been held hostage by the bomb for years. If nuclear war breaks out, it will be legal. But we're hopeful in so far as we are faithful. Having faith means we haven't given up on the world. Together, we are part of God's reign. We live as sisters and brothers. When we believe that and live accordingly, by resisting war, we generate hope.

The disarmament of our nuclear weapons needs to be

a priority for us. Peacemaking needs to be our priority. Peacemaking is not only a central characteristic of the Gospel, peacemaking is the greatest need of the world today. We are daughters and sons of God, and that means we are called to be peacemakers.

"The Christian who follows Jesus must be a nonviolent resister and revolutionary," Philip wrote in his autobiography. "There is no avoiding this truth. A Christian must take risks for the kingdom of God, the new Jerusalem. Christians are obligated to resist collusion between church and state, and to fight nonviolently against tyranny, injustice and oppression."

By the time of his death on December 6, 2002, Philip Berrigan had spent more than eleven years behind bars. "I die with the conviction, held since 1968 and Catonsville, that nuclear weapons are the scourge of the earth, that to mine them, manufacture them, deploy them, and use them is a curse against God, the human family, and the earth itself," he said in his last statement.

During the last week of his life, some thirty family members and friends gathered for a five-day vigil at Jonah House, and a new community of faith, hope, and love was formed around him. We carried his body in a homemade coffin through his inner city neighborhood to the church where he once worked as a Josephite. I presided at his funeral, and later, Bill McNichols led a prayer service that night as we buried him in the Jonah House cemetery.

This icon is based on an actual photo of Phil in chains at Danbury prison. He stands facing us, and partially blocks the bomb. As he witnesses to us from his chains, he calls us to fulfill our vocations as peacemakers, to block the bomb, to prevent its use, to abolish war, and to beat swords into plowshares. Because of his witness, we have the courage to carry on where he left off.

31 | Mary, the Triumph of the Immaculate Heart

We finish where we began, with the first witness, the first disciple, the first apostle to point to the peacemaking Christ. At Fatima, Mary urged children to pray for an end to war, and promised that, in the end, her Immaculate Heart would triumph. In this icon, she fulfills her promise, blocks the bomb, and invites us into the heart of love. In doing so, she heralds the coming of Christ's reign of nonviolence, when war, poverty, hunger, injustice, and nuclear weapons will be forever abolished so that humanity can live and breathe together in peace with justice—as her Son desires.

It is a daring witness, one that many dismiss as pious, sentimental, naïve, idealistic, if not downright impossible. But that is precisely what a Gospel witness does—point beyond the merely possible to the impossible, the coming of God's reign of peace in our hearts and throughout the world here and now. Mary invites us to join her as a witness to the nonviolent Jesus, to do our part in the global grassroots campaign for disarmament and justice, and to uphold that brilliant vision of a new world without war, injustice, or nuclear weapons.

Witnessing to the peacemaking Christ, Mary knows, is the noblest endeavor anyone can undertake. Whoever we are, wherever we are, however we live, whatever we do, we can witness to

Christ and his reign of peace, like Mary, by serving him in one another, loving one another, showing compassion to one another, practicing nonviolence toward one another, and hastening God's realm of peace in our midst and for all humanity. As we stand up against the ultimate evil—the thousands of nuclear weapons in our arsenal—we, too, block the bomb and hasten its demise.

Nuclear disarmament is not a pie-in-the-sky dream or a fairy tale for young children. Both South Africa and the Ukraine have unilaterally dismantled their nuclear arsenals. Our country developed the first atomic bomb and has brought the world to the brink of destruction through nuclear terrorism. Now it must hear the cry of the world and lead the way toward nuclear abolition. Each of us can do our part by joining Mary in praying for an end to war, refusing to cooperate with war, demanding that our nuclear arsenal be dismantled, and resisting the culture of war with the wisdom of Gospel nonviolence.

As we ponder this mysterious, powerful icon, we can pray the prayer of Pope John Paul II (written in 1999 to the Immaculate Heart of Mary), that we might join with Mary and serve as a living witness to Christ and his reign of peace and love:

> *Mary, help us to conquer the menace of evil which so easily takes root in the hearts of people of today, and whose immeasurable effects already weigh down upon our world and seem to block the paths toward the future.*
> *From famine and war, deliver us.*
> *From nuclear war, from incalculable self-destruction, from every kind of war, deliver us.*

From sins against human life from its very beginning, deliver us.

From hatred and from the demeaning of the dignity of the children of God, deliver us.

From every kind of injustice in society, both national and international, deliver us.

From readiness to trample on the commandments of God, deliver us.

From the loss of awareness of good and evil, deliver us.

From sins against the Holy Spirit, deliver us.

Accept, O Mother of Christ, this cry laden with the sufferings of all individual human beings, laden with the sufferings of whole societies.

Help us with the power of the Holy Spirit to conquer all sin: individual sin and the "sin of the world," sin in all its manifestations.

Let there be revealed once more in the history of the world the infinite saving power of the redemption, the power of merciful love.

May it put a stop to evil.

May it transform consciences.

May your Immaculate Heart reveal for all the Light of Hope.

Amen.

Closing Prayer

Lord, make me your witness.
In this world of darkness, let my light shine.
In this world of lies, let me speak the good news of your truth.
In this world of hate and fear, let me radiate your love.
In this world of despair, let me spread hope.
In this world of systemic injustice and institutionalized evil, let
me promote justice and goodness.
In this world of sadness and sorrow, let me bring joy.
In this world of cruelty and condemnation, let me show your
compassion.
In this world of vengeance and retaliation, let me offer your mercy
and reconciliation.
In this world of war, let me serve your gift of peace.
In this world of violence, make me a teacher and apostle of your
nonviolence.
In this world of death, let me proclaim the new life of
resurrection.
Help me witness to the resurrection of Jesus by loving my enemies,
showing compassion, feeding the hungry, sheltering the
homeless, serving the poor, liberating the oppressed, resisting
war, beating swords into plowshares, and disarming my heart
and the world.
In the name of the risen, nonviolent Jesus. Amen.

John Dear is a priest, pastor, and peacemaker. He is the author/editor of twenty books including *Living Peace, Jesus the Rebel, Disarming the Heart, The God of Peace, The Sound of Listening,* and *The Questions of Jesus.* He lectures on Christian peacemaking to tens of thousands of people across the country each year. He lives in northern New Mexico. For information, see: www.johndear.org.

William Hart McNichols is a priest and iconographer. He serves at the Church of St. Francis of Assisi in Taos, New Mexico. His icons have been featured in *The Bride* (by Daniel Berrigan), and *Christ All Mericful* and *Mary, Mother of All Nations* (both by Megan McKenna).